RICHARD BROME

A STUDY OF HIS LIFE AND WORKS

BY

CLARENCE EDWARD ANDREWS

ARCHON BOOKS
1972

Library of Congress Cataloging in Publication Data

Andrews, Clarence Edward, 1883–1932.
    Richard Brome.

    (Yale studies in English, v. 46)
    Reprint of the 1913 ed.
    A part of the author's thesis, Yale.
    Bibliography: p.
    1. Brome, Richard, d. 1652? I. Series.
PR2439.B5Z6 1972   822'.4   72-6665
    ISBN 0-208-01122-6

First published 1913
Reprinted 1972 with permission of
Yale University Press
in an unaltered and unabridged edition
as an Archon Book
by The Shoe String Press, Inc.
Hamden, Connecticut 06514

[Yale Studies in English, vol. 46]

Printed in the United States of America

'The cock in the fable scratched up a pearl from the dunghill, and it is possible that some ingenious student may discover pearls in what is certainly the rubbish heap of Brome's plays.'

J. A. Symonds.

PREFACE

This study is but a part of the original thesis, the title of which was *Richard Brome, a Study of his Life and Works, with an Edition of the* Antipodes, *reprinted from the Quarto of* 1640, *with Introduction, Notes, and Glossary*. The edition of the play I hope to bring out later. My aim in the present study has been, first, to bring together all the facts previously known about Brome, together with the results of research on his work up to the present time. To this material I have been able to add a considerable number of biographical details, and have made a study of his position with relation to his contemporaries, the structure of his plays, and the influences exerted upon him. To this I have added, in an appendix, a special study of one play as illustrative of the statements made about his work in general.

Though the study of Brome by my predecessor, Dr. E. K. R. Faust (Halle, 1887), is, in general, a careful piece of work, so much has been added to our knowledge of Elizabethan drama during the twenty-five years that have elapsed since the publication of his thesis, that it seemed to me the ground might be profitably surveyed again from a different point of view.

My thanks are due, first to Professor Henry A. Beers, under whom the thesis was written ; to Professors Albert S. Cook and John M. Berdan for valuable suggestions and criticisms ; to Professor Charles W. Wallace, of the University of Nebraska, for the use of some manuscript notes ; to my colleague, Professor Charles W. Cobb, for assistance with the section on Brome's versification ; and, finally, I feel especially grateful to Dr. William P.

McCune, who, while working in the same century, has given me much valuable aid all through my task.

A portion of the expense of printing this thesis has been borne by the Modern Language Club of Yale University, from funds placed at its disposal by the generosity of Mr. George E. Dimock of Elizabeth, New Jersey, a graduate of Yale in the Class of 1874.

Amherst College, Oct. 1, 1912.   C. E. A.

CONTENTS

LIFE

The palæontologist who reconstructs the skeleton of a dinosaur from two tail-vertebræ and a claw, and then from the skeleton writes a book on his habits, has a greater chance of coming near the truth than the literary historian who must base his conjectures respecting the life of his subject on the half dozen surviving references, usually to personal circumstances of more interest to the subject himself than to anybody else. Richard Brome,[1] though no Elizabethan dinosaur, has left us a few scattered fossil facts from which to reconstruct his life. Such are the early biographical sketches of Phillips (1675), Winstanley (1687), and Langbaine (1691)—all drawn chiefly from the title-pages, prefaces, and commendatory verses of Brome's plays, which, with the prologues and epilogues, still remain the principal sources of evidence. There are also two or three references in Jonson, half a dozen in contemporary works, Brome's verses prefatory to his friends' works, Sir Henry Herbert's office-book, and a single legal document.

Most of the scanty references we have concerning Richard Brome associate him with Ben Jonson. In fact, his place in literature is that of the closest and most successful follower of the great dramatist. The first mention of Brome occurs in 1614 in the Induction to *Bartholomew Fair*, where the stage-keeper says : ' But for the whole play, will you have the truth on't ?—I am looking lest the poet hear me, or his man, Master Brome, behind the arras—it is like to be a very conceited scurvy

---

[1] The fact that the form Broome sometimes occurs, and that Brome is punningly alluded to as 'sweeping,' indicates the pronunciation of the name.

one, in plain English.' Dr. Faust[1] suggests that to be called ' man ' he must have been born late in the sixteenth century. Besides this, the statements that he is ' full of age and care ' in 1640,[2] and that the *Jovial Crew*[3] (1641) is the issue of his old age, put 1590 as certainly the latest date. This is as near as it is possible to come at present to the date of his birth. His birthplace does not admit of even so much conjecture. One more reference in Jonson's works, probably not far removed from the previous one in time, shows what one of the duties of his ' man ' was, though Brome is not mentioned by name. This occurs in Epigram 101,[4] *Inviting a Friend to Supper*:

> Howsoe'er, my man
> Shall read a piece of Virgil, Tacitus,
> Livy, or of some better book to us,
> Of which we 'll speak our minds amids our meat.

This would seem to indicate that Jonson's servant was not absolutely a menial, but was either a man of some education or of such intelligence that Jonson might educate him. A parallel case is that of Nathaniel Field, the boy-actor who later became a playwright, who, Jonson told Drummond,[5] had been his scholar, and had read Horace and Martial to him.

The Rev. Ronald Bayne,[6] following a suggestion of Dr. Faust's, considers that Brome was a secretary or amanuensis[7] rather than a valet. To support this he

---

[1] E. K. R. Faust, *Richard Brome* (Halle dissertation, 1887), p. 3. Practically all that is of value in this thesis is reprinted in *Herrig's Archiv*, Vol. 82 (1889).

[2] *Court Begger*, Prologue.   [3] *Jovial Crew*, Dedication.

[4] Folio of 1616. Ben Jonson, *Works*, ed. Wheatley and Cunningham, 8. 204.

[5] *Works* 9. 379.   [6] *Cambridge Hist. Eng. Lit.* 6. 252.

[7] Colley Cibber in 1740 was the first to speak of Brome as an amanuensis (*Apology*, 4th ed., 2. 203).

cites the epigram just mentioned, and a ' sonnet of some literary merit ' prefixed to the *Northern Lass*, and signed 'St. Br.,'[1] in which the writer declares himself to be the poet's brother—a fact which should make us beware of assuming low rank for Brome. This is rather slight evidence, for, in an age in which watermen wrote verses, why might not cooks and valets ? And then, besides Jonson's address to him as his ' former servant,'[2] Alexander Brome, his friend, and the editor of his posthumous works, says :

> Poor he came into th' world.[3]

Again, in defending Richard from detractors who belittled him for his relations with Jonson, he says, in the midst of a long list of classic writers of humble origin ' nay (to instance in our *Authors* own order), Nævius the Comedian [was] a Captains mans man.' And Brome himself, in his commendatory verses in the folio of Beaumont and Fletcher (1647), says :

> Why, what are you, cry some, that prate to us ?
> Do we not know you for a flashy meteor,
> And styl'd at best the Muses' serving-creature ?
> Do you control ? Ye 've had your jeer: sirs, no;
> But in an humble manner let you know,
> Old serving-creatures oftentimes are fit
> T' inform young masters, as in land, in wit.

These passages, and others scattered through his prologues, which show that he always ' considered himself somewhat an intruder in the realm of Parnassus,' outweigh, I am inclined to think, the evidence of the fraternal

---

[1] Stephen Brome (?).
[2] See below, prefatory verses to *Northern Lass*.
[3] Prefatory verses to octavo of 1659.

' sonnet,' and the considerable knowledge of Latin shown in the plays.   Brome probably began his relations with Jonson as a witty young serving-man who interested his master to such an extent that he undertook his education, as he had already that of the young Nathaniel Field.   And this education might have been undertaken originally as much for the convenience of the master as the improvement of the servant.

Colley Cibber, in his *List of Dramatic Authors*, boldly asserts that Brome ' had his education at Eton '; but as Cibber is eleven years astray concerning the date of his death, and very carelessly misdates the publication of many of the plays, this extremely improbable and unauthoritative statement is negligible.   However, his education, wherever he got it, was quite respectable.   His English is always correct, and his vocabulary ample, with an occasional fondness for unusual Latin derivatives. His style is distinctly more colloquial than academic. But the important indication that he received some scholastic knowledge is the number and correctness of his classical quotations and allusions.   The pedant in the *City Wit*, and the curate in the *Queen and Concubine*, continually use snatches of Latin phrases that show at least a knowledge of grammar on the part of the author. Dr. Bayne thinks that these have a sprightliness and comicality which indicate that his Latin was not acquired late in life.   On the other hand, the somewhat pedantic kaleidoscope of not uncommon classical allusions in the *Court Begger*, if they indicate anything at all, suggest, I think, the opposite.   Then Brome's quotations are always very obvious, like *monstrum horrendum, hinc illæ lachrymæ*, and *Iamque opus exegi quod nec Iovis ira, nec ignis*.   The last, for instance, occurs in at least four conspicuous places in contemporary letters.   And such phrases as *non progredi est regredi, euphoniæ gratia*, or *deceptio visus* might be culled any Sunday from a sermon at St. Paul's ; while a very fair stock of mere allusions might be found in a sententious almanac. The few French phrases in the *New Academy* and the *Sparagus Garden,* although they are idiomatic and correct, of course prove nothing as to Brome's knowledge of the language, and Ward's suggestion,[1] based on two sentences in the *Novella,* that perhaps he knew a little German, is even more doubtful than that he knew French. Again, it would be very unsafe to base any conjecture concerning his connection with the profession of law on the knowledge of legal jargon shown in *Covent Garden Weeded* 2. 1, and to a slighter extent elsewhere in Brome ; for in all his works there is not half so much of this kind of lore as in a single play of Jonson's—as, for instance, the *Staple of News.* In fact, for all the special knowledge of languages and law in the plays, I think there is nothing to show more than a ready memory, and a clever ability at making a little knowledge go a long way. We may sum him up as he, or Heywood, did a character in the *Lancashire Witches*[2] :

' It seems he is a peece of a scholar.'

' What because he hath read a little Scriveners Latine, hee never proceeded farther in his Accidence than to *Mentire non est meum* ; and that was such a hard lesson to learn that he stuck at *mentire* ; and cu'd never reach to *non est meum* : since, a meere Ignaro, and not worth acknowledgment.'

A hint of Brome's training by Jonson, and of his position in the household, is given in an entry in the Herbert MS. for Oct. 2, 1623, on licensing a play[3] ' for the Princes Company (at the Red Bull). A new comedy

---

[1] *Dict. Nat. Biog.* 6. 395.   [2] Heywood, *Works* 4. 175.
[3] Fleay, *Chronicle Hist.* p. 302.

called a *Fault in Friendship*, written by young Johnson
and Broome.' This was Benjamin Jonson, Jr. of whom we
know nothing except that his father obtained the post
of Master of the Revels for him in 1635, and that he died
in November of the same year.[1] The comedy is lost, but
the record of its authorship shows that Jonson was
training Brome and his own son together in the art of
playmaking. Six years later (Feb. 9, 1629), another play
was licensed, this time by Brome alone, called the
Love-sick Maid, or the Honour of Young Ladies. This
pleased the court so well that the actors of the King's
Company on March 10 presented Herbert with 2 £ 'on its
good success.'[2]

By the date of this play Brome seems to have become a
professional playwright, and to have severed his intimate
connection with his former master. In fact, the relations
between the two seem, at least for a time, to have been
somewhat strained. The evidence for this is found in
Jonson's *Ode to Himself* written after what he considered
the failure of the *New Inn* (1629). At the end of the
octavo edition of the *New Inn* (1631) is the ode, which is
headed, *The just indignation the author tooke at the vulgar
censure of his Play, by some malicious spectators, begat
the following Ode to himself*. This edition appeared two
years after the production of the play. Another
copy of the ode appeared after Jonson's death, bound
up with his translation of the *Art of Poetry*, in 1640.
Another copy, almost identical with this second, was
discovered by Dr. G. B. Tennant[3] in Bodleian MS.
Ashmole 38, pp. 80, 81. The third stanza of the edition
of 1631 reads :

[1] *Dict. Nat. Biog.* 30. 182.
[2] Fleay, *Chronicle Hist.* p. 334.
[3] Tennant's ed. *New Inn* (Yale Studies in English, No. 34),
Introduction, pp. xxi ff.

No doubt some mouldy tale
Like *Pericles* ; and stale
As the Shrieves crusts, and nasty as his fish-
    scraps, out of every dish,
Throwne forth and rack't into the common tub,
May keepe up the *Play-club* :
There, sweepings doe as well
As the best order'd meale.
For, who the relish of these ghests will fit,
Needs set them, but, the almes-basket of wit.

The other two copies have for lines 7 and 8:

Broomes sweeping(s) doe as well
Thear as his Masters Meale.

Gifford's explanation of the difference in the versions is :
' There seems to have existed a wish among the poet's
friends to embroil him with his old servant, Richard
Brome : it was, however, without effect, for the envious
Ben continued to esteem him to the close of his life.'
Gifford then brings in evidence the fact that Jonson
wrote prefatory verses for the *Northern Lass* in 1632,
which I shall quote presently. He says, further, in his
note on these verses printed in *Underwoods*, No. 28[1]:
' I have already noticed the attempts of Randolph and
others to create a feeling of hostility in our poet towards
Brome. That they met with no success is evident ; for
Jonson always remained warmly attached to his old and
meritorious servant, and Brome continued no less grateful,' etc. Ward[2] follows Gifford in this point, but Fleay[3]
declares ' Broomes sweepings ' to be undoubtedly the
original reading, which was altered in the published
edition. He says Jonson ' was jealous of his dead master,
Shakespeare, and his living faithful servant, Brome.'

---

[1] *Works* 8. 342.
[2] Ward, *Hist. Eng. Dram. Lit.* 3. 126, and *Dict. Nat. Biog.*
[3] *Biog. Chron.* 1. 352.

Dr. Tennant,[1] I think, has proved Fleay's statement
correct without much doubt.   His reasons for believing
in the priority of the version of MS. Ashmole 38 and 1640
over that of 1631 are, first, that the last stanza in the
latter is unquestionably improved in structure.   Second-
ly, the use of the word ' sweepings ' is utterly flat without
a reference to Brome.   Thirdly, there is a very good reason
for Jonson's anger to be found in the fact that Brome's
Love-sick Maid, which was such a great success, was
produced only three weeks after the failure of the *New Inn*.
And, finally, most of the replies to the ode seem to indicate
that the authors saw in MS. the copy that contained the
reading, ' Broomes sweepings.'   Dr. Tenannt sums up
the whole question as follows : ' With such facts before
one, how easy it is to understand the mention of ' Broomes
sweepings ' in Jonson's *Ode*, on the supposition that it
was written while illness and the sting of failure combined
to make him express resentment at the success of one he
knew was his inferior ; and how natural it was that when
two years had worn off the bitterness of such an experience, he should be unwilling to perpetuate the abuse
of his old servant.'

It is undoubtedly to this temporary estrangement of
Jonson and Brome that Alexander Brome alludes in his
verses prefatory to the *Jovial Crew*[2] (1652) :

> I *love thee* for . . . .
> Thy *luck* to *please* so well : who could go faster ?
> At first to be the *Envy* of thy *Master*.

Randolph's reply to Jonson's *Ode*, alluded to above,
contains the following reference to Brome[3] :

[1] Ed. *New Inn*, Introduction.
[2] R. Brome, *Works* (1873) 3. 349.
[3] Randolph, *Poems* (1875) 2. 582.

And let those things in plush,
Till they be taught to blush,
Like what they will, and more contented be
With that Broome swept from thee.

And Carew's reply, though not so direct, may have intended Brome by the person[1]

Who hath his flock of cackling geese compared
To thy tuned choir of swans.

Carew says further :

Thy labour'd works shall live, when time devours
Th' abortive offspring of their hasty hours.
Thou art not of their rank.

Two more recollections of this ill-feeling appeared in *Jonsonus Virbius*[2] (1638). One of these, signed I. C.,[3] says :

Let him who daily steales
From thy most precious meales
(Since thy strange plenty finds no loss by it)
Feed himself with the fragments of thy wit.

This I suppose to be Brome. At any rate the ' grosse base stuffe ' in the next stanza is doubtless intended to include his work. The other, by R. Brideoake, I shall quote more at length :

And though thy fancies were too high for those
That but aspire to Cockpit-flight, or prose,
Though the fine plush and velvets of the age
Did oft for sixpence damn thee from the stage,
And with their mast and acorn stomachs ran
To the nasty sweepings of thy serving man,
Before thy cates, and swore thy stronger food,
'Cause not by them digested, was not good.

The not unnatural resentment and jealousy of Jonson, which had given rise to all these bitter comments in verse, seems to have completely disappeared by 1632. In that year Brome's first publication, the very successful *Northern Lass,* came out with six copies of prefatory verses, headed by the following from Jonson[1] :

To my old Faithful Servant, and (by his continued Vertue) my loving Friend, the Author of this Work, **Mr.** *Richard Brome.*

I Had you for a Servant, once, Dick Brome;
  And you performed a Servants faithful parts.
Now, you are got into a nearer room,
  Of Fellowship, *professing my old Arts.*
And you do doe them well with good applause,
  Which you have justly gained from the Stage,
By observation of those Comick Lawes
  Which I, your Master, *first did teach the Age.*
You learn'd it well, and for it serv'd your time
  A Prentice-ship : *which few doe now adays.*
Now each Court-Hobby-horse will wince in rime ;
  Both learned and unlearned all write Playes.
It was not so of old : *Men took up trades*
  That knew the Crafts they had bin bred in right :
An honest Bilbo-*Smith would make good blades,*
  And the Physician teach men spue or shite ;
The Cobler *kept him to his nall, but now*
  He 'll be a Pilot, *scarse can guide a Plough.*
                                                    Ben. Johnson.

The latter part of these verses is doubtfully complimentary, but what would be an insult from an ordinary individual might be intended as a mark of extreme graciousness from Ben. At any rate they seem to have been so construed by Brome, who, whenever he refers to his master, is ever grateful and loyal. How close the relations between the two were from this time on till Jonson's death it is impossible to say. Brome is never alluded to

[1] Brome, *Works* 3. ix ; also Ben Jonson, *Works* 8. 342.

as a ' Son of Ben ' by any of his contemporaries, but of
course very few of the circle of young men about Jonson
are actually so called.

The ' Sons of Ben ' probably never existed as a definitely organized club, but were merely a number of men
with a common interest in Jonson, whose powerful
personality easily attracted and dominated. I think it
doubtful whether all of them even knew one another.
The term ' son ' in the seventeenth century was a somewhat vague evidence of friendship and approval ex-
hibited towards a young man by one considerably older.
Many instances of this can be found. For example,
the prologue at a revival of Beaumont and Fletcher's
Custom of the Country[1] (between 1635 and 1642) was
spoken by ' my son Clark,' an actor ; Nathaniel Field
addresses an urgent appeal for 40 £ to ' Father Henchlowe '
(Henslowe)[2] ; Massinger wrote lines to his ' son,' Sam
Smith, upon his *Minerva*[3] ; and Dekker wrote verses
' to my Sonne Broom.'[4]   The explanation of this custom
offered by Sir Harris Nicolas, that it was a practice
which originated among the alchemists,[5] I think, rather
far fetched, for it is a quite natural way of showing
affection or respect, and one that might arise without any
precedent.[6]

It has become customary to allude to the dozen or so
of young men who modeled their work in the lyric or the
drama on Jonson's, as his ' sons.'   Though we have evidence that there was a personal friendship between most
of them and Jonson, and, in some cases, friendships among

---

[1] *Works* (1844) 4. 390, note c.   [2] *Dict. Nat. Biog.* 18. 409.
[3] *Wit Restored* (1658), ed. J. C. Hotten, London, n. d., p. 262.
[4] Before *Northern Lass :* Brome's *Works* 3. xi.
[5] *Complete Angler*, ed. Sir H. Nicolas, 2. 323, n.
[6] In *Covent Garden Weeded* (3. 1. p. 39), Capt. Driblow calls his
band of ' roarers ' ' sons '.

themselves, there are but seven of these admirers whom
I find definitely alluded to as ' sons.' Howell,[1] Love-
lace,[2] and Marmion [3] call Jonson ' father,' or speak of
themselves as ' son.' Randolph has a poem called,
*A Gratulatory to Mr. Ben Johnson, for adopting him to be
his sonne,*[4] and the story of his being received by Jonson
as such is told in an apocryphal jest-book[5] a century
later. Jonson calls Joseph Rutter ' my Dear Son, and
Right Learned Friend.'[6] Aubrey[7] relates an anecdote of
a certain wit, named John Hoskyns, who desired to be
adopted by the elder poet. And, finally, Humphrey
Mosely, the publisher, quotes Jonson as saying ' my son
Cartwright writes all like a man.'[8] These are all the
definite references I have found. There are, besides, two
poems in *Underwoods—an Epigram to a Friend and Son,*[9]
and *An Epistle Answering to one that asked to be sealed of
the tribe of Ben*[10]—and Falkland's reference to Jonson's
' adopted children.'[11] There is nothing here indicative
even of a literary club, and the *Verses placed over the Door
at the Entrance into the Apollo,*[12] Jonson's favorite room
at the Devil Tavern, as well as the *Leges Conviviales,*[13] lead
one to think that the 'Sons of Ben' who met there with him
did it more for the joy in life, and the pleasure of repartee,
than for serious literary criticism and mutual improvement.

[1] *Epistolæ Ho-Elianæ,* ed. Jacobs, 1. 267, 276, 322 ; 2. 376.
[2] *On Sanazar, Poems,* ed. Hazlitt, p. 240.
[3] *Jonsonus Virbius* : Ben Jonson, *Works* 9. 465.
[4] *Works,* ed. Hazlitt, 2. 537.
[5] *Ben Jonson's Jests, or the Wit's Pocket Companion,* London, 1751.
[6] Prefatory verses to the *Shepherd's Holiday* : Ben Jonson,
Works 9. 336.
[7] *Brief Lives,* ed. Clark, 1. 417.
[8] Cartwright's *Poems* (1651), Preface.
[9] *Works* 8. 446.   [10] *Works* 8. 416.
[11] *Jonsonus Virbius* : Ben Jonson, *Works* 9. 426.
[12] *Works* 9. 73.   [13] *Works* 9. 67.

The allusions to the Apollo in the *Staple of News*, in Herrick's poem, and in Marmion's *Fine Companion*, bear out the idea that it was a place for glorious bacchanalian revels.

As none of the men definitely called the ' Sons of Ben,' with the exception of Shakerley Marmion, are known to have had any relations with Brome, it is quite possible that he did not find himself wholly welcome ' to the Oracle of Apollo' among the rather aristocratic circle. Perhaps, however, the mere existence or non-existence of complimentary verses is too slight a ground for such a conjecture.

Whatever his relations with his contemporary poets and playwrights may have been, he was undoubtedly becoming a most successful rival. We have already seen that one of his plays was produced at court by the King's Company in 1629. He seems to have continued his relations with them until 1635, and had his plays[1] put on at the Globe and Blackfriars during the period between those dates, at the same time that that company was playing many of the masterpieces of Fletcher, Massinger, and Ford. The latter part of Brome's work for the King's Men seems to have consisted in rewriting at least three old plays of Heywood.[2]

In 1635 he was evidently considered such a success as a dramatist that the King's Revels Company ventured to make a three-year contract with him. This has been unearthed by Professor Wallace, of the University of Nebraska, in his search for Shakespearean documents. I quote from one of his articles[3] : ' Richard Brome in 1635 made a contract with the Salisbury Court Theatre to write three plays a year for three years at a salary

---

[1] For a probable list of extant plays written during this period see Chronology, below.

[2] Fleay, *Biog. Chron.* 1. 301.

[3] 'Shakspere and the Blackfriars,' *Century*, Vol. 80 (September 1910).

of 15 shillings a week, plus the first day's profits from each new play as a benefit. In 1638 it was agreed that the contract should be continued seven years longer, at 20 shillings a week for Brome's exclusive services. But the rival theatre, the Cockpit, lured him away with a better offer, and the new contract was not signed. The most interesting items here are the limit of three plays a year, and special provision that Brome should not be allowed to publish any of his own plays without the consent of the company.' The discovery of this document is not only an extremely important addition to our knowledge of Brome, but a most significant contribution to stage-history. It shows us much as to the relation of a popular playwright to the company for which he was writing.

Professor Wallace has been so generous as to send me some further facts regarding this contract, from his hitherto unpublished notes. He states that Brome, previous to the contract, was with the Red Bull Company.[1] The contract is dated July 20, 1635. The amount of the benefit of the first night on one occasion was estimated at 5 £ or upwards. Brome was to give his exclusive services to the company. One play he wrote for them, the *Sparagus Garden*, was so popular that the estimated profits to the company were 1000 £. In the three years during which Brome was writing for the Salisbury Court Theatre, he had written, besides numerous songs, epilogues, and revisions of scenes in revived plays, but six of the nine plays agreed on in the contract. He had also written a play or two for the Cockpit, contrary to contract.

---

[1] This indicates that Brome must have been connected with two companies at the same time, for in 1634 he was writing for the King's Men, who were playing at the Globe and Blackfriars (see Chronology). There is no other evidence that he was connected with the Red Bull Company after 1623.

Though Professor Wallace states in the article quoted above that the second contract was not signed, he writes me that Brome, on this new contract, which is dated August, 1638, delivered one play the following winter after Christmas, and another before Easter, 1639, which the company refused to accept. ' Then he went to the Cockpit with Beeston, where he met with better favor, about which details are not given.'

Further light is thrown on these facts by the curious note appended to the *Antipodes* in the quarto of 1640. It reads : ' Courteous Reader, *You shal find in this Book more than was presented upon the* Stage, and *left out of the* Presentation, *for Superfluous length (as some of the* Players pretended) *I thought it good al should be inserted according to the allowed* Original ; *and as it was, at first, intended for the* Cockpit Stage, *in the right of my most deserving Friend Mr.* William Beeston, *unto whom it properly appertained ; and so I leave it to thy perusal, as it was generallly applauded, and well acted at* Salisbury Court. *Farewell*, Ri. Brome.'

What evidently happened was that Brome, late in 1637,[1] before the expiration of his contract with the Salisbury Court Theatre, wrote the *Antipodes* for the newly formed King and Queen's Young Company, or Beeston's Boys.[2] The Salisbury Court Company forced Brome to give the play to them, because he had delivered but six of the nine plays promised, and had guaranteed his exclusive services. The following passage in the *Court Begger* (1640) (2. 1, p. 215) seems to indicate that the company brought suit against him: ' Here's a trim business towards, and as idle as the players going to Law with their Poets.'

[1] See Chronology, below, p. 36.
[2] J. T. Murray (*English Dramatic Companies* 1. 367) says the company was formed shortly before Feb. 7, 1637, and played at the Cockpit.

The fact that the Salisbury Court Theatre, in spite of Brome's failing to furnish his full quota of plays, made such a liberal offer for the renewal of the contract before the trouble that I have just discussed, indicates that the plays written under the first three-year arrangement must have been very successful. Among them are, if our chronology is correct, *Queen and Concubine, Sparagus Garden, Mad Couple well Matched, English Moor,* and *Damoiselle.* As the lost play, *Wit in a Madness,* was entered in the Stationers' Register March 19, 1639/40, along with the *Sparagus Garden* and the *Antipodes,* it is possibly of the same period of composition. Two other lost plays, *Christianetta* and *Jewish Gentleman,* entered the same year, admit of no conjecture as to the date of composition.

Some of the plays just mentioned as written for the Revels Company at Salisbury Court must have passed to the Queen's Company when it absorbed the Revels in 1637, just before the expiration of Brome's first contract. The history of the transference of plays at this time is extremely confusing and doubtful. Two of the plays went to Beeston's Boys after they were organized— the *Mad Couple*[1] and the *Antipodes.*[2] All the plays of this period were first produced at Salisbury Court.

The only extant plays that were written for Beeston's Boys seem to be the *Court Begger* (c. 1640)[3] and the *Jovial Crew*[4] (1641). We may presume that, during the three years he was with this company before the elosing

---

[1] J. T. Murray, *op. cit.* 1. 369.

[2] J. P. Collier, *Hist. Eng. Dram. Poetry* 3. 139.

[3] Not 1632, as the title-page states. Fleay (*Biog. Chron.* 1. 40) is undoubtedly right in this correction.

[4] Fleay (*ibid.*) says it was acted by 'their Majesties' servants.' He may mean the King and Queen's Young Company, the official title of Beeston's Boys, who were the only company at the Cockpit from 1637—1642.

of the theatres in 1642, he wrote other plays that have been since lost.

We have one more glimpse of him during this period, when we find him editing, apparently as a labor of love,[1] the first edition of Fletcher's *Monsieur Thomas*, which appeared in quarto in 1639, with a dedication to Charles Cotton.

Between the time that Brome was deprived of the opportunity to pursue his calling by the downfall of things theatrical in 1642 and his death about 1652, we have but three references to him. One is his long poem in praise of Fletcher, which appeared among the verses of admirers in the folio of Beaumont and Fletcher's works in 1647. Two years later he contributed to the *Lachrymæ Musarum*, a collection of elegies in memory of Henry, Lord Hastings, and in all probability was the R. B.[2] who edited the volume. Other contributors to this volume were the Earl of Westmorland, Lord Falkland, Sir Aston Cokayne, Charles Cotton, Herrick, Denham, Marvell, Alexander Brome, J. Bancroft, and the young Dryden, who here appeared in print for the first time.

In 1652 Brome published the very popular *Jovial Crew*, undoubtedly his best play. The dedication to Thomas Stanley shows that the old dramatist had fallen on evil days. He says fortune has made him a beggar, but he is '*poor and proud*.' '*You know, Sir, I am old, and cannot* cringe, *nor* Court *with the powder'd and ribbanded Wits of our daies*. . . . The Times conspire to make us all Beggers.' If forty shillings were still the price of a dedication,[3] Brome must have found other means of

[1] See Dedication and Prefatory Verses.

[2] A break in the pagination and an added note show that Brome's verses were to be placed last, as the volume was originally planned. See *Grolier Club Catalogue,* and Corser.

[3] Field, *A Woman is a Weathercock,* Dedication (1612) ; see also below, p. 24.

livelihood at this period of his misfortune and decline. In the above mentioned dedication he hints at favors from his patron. This may suggest possible aid. His condition must have been much the same as that mentioned in the *Actor's Remonstrance*[1] (1643) : ' For some of our ablest ordinary Poets instead of their annuall stipends and beneficiall second-dayes, being for meere necessitie compelled to get a living by writing contemptible penny pamphlets in which they have not so much as poeticall license to use any attribute of their profession but that of *Quidlibet audendi* ? and faining miraculous stories and relations of unheard of battels.'

The publication of the *Jovial Crew* is the last we hear of Brome during his lifetime. The following year, 1653, Alexander Brome, who edited *Five New Plays*, says in his preface : ' *for the* Author *bid me tell you that, now that he is dead, he is of* Falstaffs *minde, and cares not for* Honour.' We may therefore place the date of his death as 1652 or 1653. The same editor, who brought out five more plays in 1659, refers with some pathos to the poverty in which he died :

> He was his own *Executor*, and made
> Ev'n with the world ; and that small *All* he had—
> He without *Law* or *Scribe* put out of doubt;
> *Poor* he came into th' world and *poor* went out.
> His *soul* and *body* higher powers claim.
> There 's nothing left to play with, but his *name*;
> Which you may freely *toss*; he all endures.
> But as you use his name, so 'll others yours.

Beside these facts about Brome's career proper, a number of hints in regard to his literary relationships are furnished by prefaces and commendatory verses, which the imaginative student will find to supply bases for

---

[1] Ed. Hazlitt, 264.

indefinite conjecture. This, I fear, is rather shaky ground, for the *littérateur* of the sevententh century, I fancy, often responded to the request for prefatory verses in much the same manner as one might subscribe to worthy charities ˙which bore one. Many of the hundred odd gentlemen who acceded to Tom Coryat's request for verses to print before his *Crudities* were the merest acquaintances, who did not scruple to take any opportunity to make fun of Coryat and his curious work for twenty-five years after. Such verses, therefore, seem to me rather slight evidence of friendship. However, some of the contributions to the publications of Brome during his lifetime, and immediately after, may, taken with other facts, lead us to a few conclusions.

Besides Jonson, the most important of the older generation of literary men with whom Brome had relations was Dekker. His verses before the *Northern Lass* (1632), sufficiently uninteresting in themselves, are addressed ' to my Sonne Broom and his Lasse,' and begin :

> Which, then of Both shall I commend ?
> Or thee (that art my Son and Friend)
> Or Her, by thee begot ?

Langbaine's remark[1] that Brome was a friend of Dekker, and ' always stil'd him by the title of *Father*,' was probably based on these very verses. But we have a much stronger evidence of some connection between the two men in the fact that Brome shows the influence of Dekker's work to a certain degree. This will be taken up under the consideration of Brome as a dramatist. The friendship of Brome with two mutual enemies like Jonson and Dekker need not be wondered at, for the War of the Theatres, which happened in 1601,

---

[1] *Account of the Eng. Dram. Poets* (1691), p. 121.

was so far forgotten in 1604 that Jonson was then collaborating with Marston,[1] with whom he had been quite as much at odds as with Dekker.

That Brome was well acquainted with Fletcher is evident from his lines to Fletcher's memory in the folio of 1647. After a long and humorously humble introduction on the subject of how he dares appear in the company of the great, he says of Fletcher[2]:

> You that have known him, know
> The common talk that from his lips did flow,
> And ran at waste, did savour more of wit
> Than any of his time, or since, have writ,
> But few excepted, in the stage's way:
> His scenes were acts, and every act a play.
> I knew him in his strength; even then when he,
> That was the master of his art and me,
> Most knowing Jonson, proud to call him son,
> In friendly envy swore he had out-done
> His very self: I knew him till he died.

Besides these verses, the editorship of *Monsieur Thomas,* already mentioned, substantiates the existence of a friendship between the two men.

John Ford, in his verses before the *Northern Lass,* calls himself ' The Author's very Friend,' and there is a possibility that Brome found a few suggestions in Ford's work. The author of these verses, however, may have been the John Ford of Gray's Inn, a cousin of the dramatist, to whom Tatham, Brome's friend, dedicated a book. But the fact that the dramatist contributed to *Jonsonus Virbius* shows that he was a friend of Jonson, and thus makes the chances about even either way.

With Heywood I find no indication of any relation, for the plays registered as by Brome and Heywood are doubt-

---

[1] In *Eastward Hoe.*
[2] Beaumont and Fletcher, *Works* 1. lxv.

less the result of rewriting old plays, rather than of collaboration. Shirley addresses him as his 'worthy Friend,' and generously praises his work for the knowledge of men shown in it, far more than that of University wits like Cartwright, against whom he directs a sly shaft.[1] Sir Aston Cokayne, a wealthy University man, the friend of Massinger, and a dramatist himself, wrote verses for *Five New Plays* the year after Brome's death. This, if we may judge from the verses themselves, he did probably more for the editor's sake than because of any friendship for the departed playwright.

There seems, moreover, to have been a circle of the smaller literary men of the time who frequently exchanged with one another the courtesy of writing complimentary lines. Brome contributed some to Shakerley Marmion's *Cupid and Psyche* (1637), Thomas Jordan's *Poetical Varieties* (1637), and John Tatham's *Fancies Theatre* (1640). Tatham, in return, contributed to the *Jovial Crew*, and Tatham's volume is dedicated to John Ford of Gray's Inn, who is mentioned above as possibly the author of the verses before the *Northern Lass*. Robert Chamberlain contributed both to Tatham's book and to the *Antipodes*. The C. G. in the *Antipodes*, the *Sparagus Garden*, and Tatham's *Fancies Theatre*, is in all probability Charles Gerbier.[2] F. T., Mag. Art. Oxon., who did

---

[1] *Jovial Crew* (1652). Cartwright's volume, with its many prefatory verses, appeared the year before.

[2] A C. G. wrote prefatory verses to Nabbes's *Unfortunate Mother* (also printed 1640). Bullen (ed. Nabbes 2. 88), following Hazlitt, conjectures Charles Gerbier, author of *Eulogium Heroinum* (1651) and other works. Allibone credits him with *Astrologo-Mastix* (1646) and the *Praise of Worthy Women* (1651). C. G. is also found attached to verses in Rawlin's *Rebellion* (1640), and C. Gerbier to others in John Tatham's *Fancies Theatre*, along with some by Nabbes, Brome, and Chamberlain. The lines before the *Unfortunate Mother* refer to the *New Inn*, and show Gerbier to be an admirer

two sets of verses for the *Jovial Crew*, is likely to be the same author who appears in the first edition of *Cupid and Psyche*, as Francis Tuckyr, but in later editions as F. T.[1] The J. B. in the *Jovial Crew* I cannot identify, but the same initials appear in the *Poetical Varieties*. The R. W. of the *Sparagus Garden* (1640) may (as a wild guess) be the Richard West who appears in *Jonsonus Virbius* (1638). John Hall,[2] another contributor to the *Jovial Crew*, was a clever University man, a poet and pamphleteer, a friend of Shirley and of Thomas Stanley. Thomas Nabbes, who next to Shirley was Brome's strongest rival in the comedy of manners or humors, seems to have written no verses for Brome, though he contributed to the volumes of most of the others of this group. Brome prefixed verses to Nabbes' *Microcosmus* in 1637. This interchange of literary compliments suggests that Brome may have made one of a circle of eight or ten very obscure authors that existed just before the outbreak of the war.

In the case of none of these men can we find any indication of a real friendship for Brome. The one exception to this is Alexander Brome,[3] an attorney and popular royalist poet, a man of no mean ability. His name is found attached, among those of the friends of Jonson, to a great deal of eulogistic verse. His poem, *The Club*, and his translation of the *Leges Conviviales*, show that he was often to be found among the witty revelers at the Devil Tavern. His encomiastic verses prefixed to the *Jovial Crew* seem to me to be the only ones that indicate any personal affection for the old author.

of Jonson. Fleay (*Biog. Chron.* 2. 169) says that the C. G. who prefixed verses to Rawlin's *Rebellion* was 'unquestionably Christopher Goad, not Charles Gerbier,' but his chief reason, I fancy, is that Bullen thinks otherwise.

[1] *Minor Caroline Poets*, ed. Saintsbury, 2. 7.
[2] 1627–1656.   [3] 1620–1666.

But though I may not *praise* ; I hope, I may
Be bold to *love* thee. And the *World* shall say
I've *reason* for't. *I love thee* for thy *Name;*
I love thee for thy *Merit,* and thy *Fame:*
I love thee for thy *neat* and *harmlesse wit,*
Thy *Mirth* that does so *cleane* and *closely hit.*
Thy *luck* to *please* so well : who could go faster ?
At first to be the *Envy* of thy *Master.*
I love thee for thy *self* ; for who can choose
But like the *Fountain* of so brisk a *Muse* ?
I love this *Comedie,* and every *line,*
Because tis *good,* as well 's because tis *thine.*

But the evidence of Alexander Brome's devotion to his
friend does not rest on these lines alone. It is to him
as editor that we owe the preservation of ten plays.
In 1653 he put out five, with a preface and two sets of
verses to introduce them, and in 1659 five more. This
second volume has as preface an appreciation of Brome's
work, defending him from detractors, and incidentally
praising Jonson, the master of both writers. In his verses
that follow after those of T. S. (Thomas Stanley), he states
that he is not related to Richard in ' *parts* or *person,*'
and shows some feeling in his concluding lines on the
poverty in which his friend died.[1]

The Stephen Brome who calls himself a brother to
Richard has already been spoken of. Besides him, there
was a Henry Brome, a bookseller ' at the Inn in St. Pauls
Churchyard, near the west end,' who published the
Queen's Exchange in 1657, with a brief preface. He also
had a hand in the volume of 1659, published Alexander
Brome's *Songs and Other Poems* in 1661, and as late as
1674 put out the *Westminster Drollery.* There is no
indication of relationship.

Both the volumes published by Alexander appeared

[1] Quoted above, p. 3.

without dedications, the earlier with some witty remarks on the fact that the patron must pay ' two or three pieces ' for a book which any one else may get for ' half a crown.' Richard, however, seems to have held less independent views on the practice, or needed his forty shillings more. The *Northern Lass* (1632) is addressed ' To the Right Worthy, and no lesse Judicious than Ingenious Gentleman, Richard Holford, Esquire.' If this worthy had any other virtues they have been interred with him, for I can find no other mention of his name. The only fact that appears in the dedication is that Brome received ' real favors ' from him. The *Sparagus Garden* (1640) is dedicated to William, Earl (afterward Duke) of Newcastle, ' Governour to the Prince his Highnesse.' The duke, besides gaining distinction in his political career, and some praise as an author, deserves the reputation of being the greatest literary patron of his time. Clarendon[1] says that his generalship was impaired because ' he had a tincture of a romantic spirit, and had the misfortune to have somewhat of the poet in him.' Langbaine praised him for what Clarendon considers a fault and calls him ' our English Mæcenas.' The duke and his very literary duchess took the greatest interest in Jonson, who seems to have accepted and appreciated their patronage. Jonson wrote epitaphs, elegies, appreciative verses, an interlude for a christening, and two masques at a royal entertainment for the duke. The remark of the duke, quoted in one of the duchess's letters,[2] that ' he never heard any one read well but Jonson ' suggests that the poet's relations were extremely intimate and friendly, and Jonson shows in his letters[3] that he considered the duke a munificent patron. Shirley

---

[1] *Rebellion and Civil War* 8. 82.
[2] Gifford's Life, in Ben Jonson, *Works* 1. xvi.
[3] *Works* 3. 459.

and Dryden were not merely his friends, but collaborators,[1] and Ford,[2] Jasper Mayne,[2] and Shadwell[1] dedicated works to him. Flecknoe,[1] Davenant,[1] and the philosopher Hobbes,[2] were also among those who received favors. We have no means of knowing how intimate Brome was with Newcastle. The servility of his dedication is purely a literary convention, from which it is unsafe to draw inferences. The verses, ' To my Lord of Newcastle on his Play called the Variety,' are as extravagant as all of their type, but the statement, ' He having commanded to give him my true opinion of it,' which is appended, must indicate, if true, that his lordship thought enough of Brome to ask for his judgment.[3]

William Seymour, Earl of Hertford, to whom the *Antipodes* (1640) is dedicated, seems to have had no other relation with Brome than that of patron of this work. In 1652 the *Jovial Crew*, the last play printed during the author's lifetime, was addressed to Thomas Stanley, Esq. Stanley was of the seventeenth-century type of gentleman, of broad culture, profound learning, and many interests. In addition to his long authoritative history of philosophy, he wrote several volumes of notes on Greek dramatists, and a thin collection of original poems.[4] He was also known as a patron of several minor literary men, and seems to have been a close friend of Alexander Brome. In the octavo of 1659 there is a long commendatory poem to Richard, the most detailed and appreciative eulogy that the dramatist's

---

[1] Firth, Preface to edition of the duchess's Letters.

[2] *Dict. Nat. Biog.*

[3] These verses are to be found in the octavo volume of 1659, immediately preceding *Covent Garden Weeded.*

[4] *Thomas Stanley : His Original Lyrics, complete in their collated readings of* 1647, 1651, 1657, edited with notes and introduction by L. I. Guiney, Hull, 1907.

work has received. The signature, T. S., is interpreted
by Ward in the *Dictionary of National Biography* as
Thomas Shadwell, but this attribution is quite unsuppor-
ted. I think there is no doubt that the verses are by
Stanley, not only from the fact of the previous dedication,
and his friendship with Alexander, the editor, but also
from the following lines in an *Epistle to T. S.*, later explained as Stanley, in Alexander Brome's Poems (1661)[1]:

> A poem I have sent thee heere,
> That dyes if thou shouldst be severe.
> And cause I've none worth sending down
> I've bought one cost me half a crown.
> And Dick Brome's plays which good must be
> Because they were approved by thee.

Now that we have discussed what evidence there is for
Brome's friendships, we may give some consideration to
his enmities. In the *Musarum Deliciæ* (p. 68), a collection of facetious verse published in 1656, there is an
unsigned piece entitled *Upon Aglaura printed in Folio*,
which also appears in the *Five New Plays*[2] of 1659, with
the initials R. B. added. This is a rather good bit of
satire on Suckling's *Aglaura*, which was published in a
sumptuous folio edition with wide margins in 1638. This
uncommon format for a commonplace tragi-comedy gave
the author of the satire a chance to display his wit very
cleverly in the fashionable conceited style, comparing
the text on the page, among other things, to a child lodged
in the great bed at Ware. The including of the piece
among Brome's plays by an editor who was a close friend
may be taken as evidence of authorship. As Dr. Faust
has suggested, for Brome to satirize Suckling, who had
ridiculed Jonson, in the *Session of the Poets*, was consistent
with his loyalty to his former master. Immediately

[1] P. 169. [2] Preceding *Covent Garden Weeded.*

following this poem in the same volume of 1659 is another of eight lines, called *A Song*,[1] two verses of which are :

> Nor sorrow, nor care can crosse our delights
> Nor witches, nor goblins, nor Buttery sprights,

which Dr. Faust considers a reference to Suckling's *Goblins*, or possibly to Randolph's *Amyntas*. This poem, however, is not at all satirical.

The scholar just quoted has a further conjecture as to the relations of Brome and Randolph which should be discussed.[2] *Amyntas, or the Impossible Dowry*,[3] has, as one of its *dramatis personæ*, ' Bromius, a blunt clown,' who is called in one of the scenes of horse-play a ' profane, rude groom.' I think, however, if one reads further in the play than the *dramatis personæ*, the identification of Bromius with Brome appears impossible. The character is merely an uninteresting clown. He is the ' man ' of ' Jocastus, a fantastical shepherd and a fairy knight,' who is an absurd creature that devises strange masques, and dances a morris for the entertainment of the king of the fairies. Now if Randolph is ridiculing Brome, he must also be satirizing Jonson, his own master and friend. And further, the only indication of intended satire, the pointless similarity of the names, can easily be explained away by the fact that Bromius is a very common name for Dionysus in Greek drama ; and one of the derivations of the name, which makes it mean ' the brawler,' is quite appropriate for the low-comedy shepherd in Randolph's pastoral.

As the few external allusions left to us do not help us to judge the character of Richard Brome, we must construct

---

[1] The last two verses of this occur again in the *Jovial Crew* 5, p. 445.

[2] Faust, *op. cit.*, p. 9.

[3] Written before 1635, says Schelling.

it from hints scattered through his work.   It seems to have impressed every one who has written of him in much the same way.   Ward,[1] judging from the prologues and epilogues, has expressed it very well.   He says : ' He exhibits an amusing mixture of modesty and self-consciousness as a dramatic writer.   He repeatedly begs his audience not to expect more than they will find; all he pretends to is ' but Mirth and Sense[2] ; he is content to term himself a ' Playmaker,' without aspiring as yet to the names of ' Author, or Poet,' any more than to the office of Laureate[3] ; ' a little wit, less learning, no poetry ' is all he dare boast [4] ; but though he ' scarse ever durst rank himself above the worst of Poets,' ' most that he has writ has past the rest, and found good approbation of the best '[5]; and though he only professes to help to keep alive ' the weakest branch of the stage '—that species of comedy which treats of ' low and home-bred subjects '— he questions whether it is in truth the weakest, or whether it be not

> as hard a labour for the Muse
> To Move the Earth as to dislodge a Star.[6]

This same contradiction in character occurs over and over again in Brome's prologues, epilogues, and his lines to Fletcher.   One other trait that appears is an almost Jonsonian bluff scorn of flattery and compliment[7]; but this does not seem to represent a usual mood.   In his offering of his last two plays to the public, the humility of tone seems more real, and the aged dramatist throws himself on the mercy of his audience and his patron with some show of genuine feeling.[8]   In spite of the fact that he is

---

[1] *Hist. Eng. Dram. Lit.* 3. 127.   [2] *Novella*, Prologue.
[3] *Damoiselle*, Prologue.   [4] *Love-Sick Court*, Prologue.
[5] *Queen's Exchange*, Prologue.   [6] *Antipodes*, Prologue.
[7] *Mad Couple*, Prologue.
[8] *Court Begger*, Prologue and Epilogue.

usually guilty of the mortal sin of spiritual pride in his boastful excessive modesty, we are told by his friend Alexander Brome[1] that he was a devout believer : 'One he adored and all the rest defied.'[2] This, however, says Ward,[3] was not inconsistent with his hatred of Scotch Presbyterians,[4] and of Puritans in general.

There is a considerable amount of evidence to show that Brome was an extremely popular playwright in his day. Though none of it taken individually can be considered conclusive, the whole body of it will bear some weight. The statements of many of the title-pages to the plays, Brome's own dedications[5] and prologues,[6] and the verses of Jonson and other friends,[7] all agree in giving us the impression that the confidence in Brome's power to please the public that is implied in the two offered contracts with Salisbury Court was well justified. The fact is worth considering, too, that fifteen plays of a man of very obscure origin were published within seven years after his death. The stationer's preface to the last volume of five plays states that the first had sold well, but this may be taken *cum grano*. Finally, a remark in the epilogue to the *Court Begger* shows that he received the best price for his plays from the actors, ' because we would ha' the best.' But in spite of this general approval, there seem to be also suggestions of adverse criticism in the commendatory verses of friends who hasten to deny the charges intimated. The four[8] references on which I base this may be considered merely as examples of a literary convention

[1] *Jovial Crew*, Dedication.   [2] *Five Plays*, 1653, Preface.
[3] *Dict. Nat. Biog.*   [4] *Court Begger.*   [5] E. g., *Northern Lass.*
[6] Especially the broad statement in Prologue to *Queen's Exchange*.
[7] E. g., Tatham and A. Brome in *Jovial Crew.*
[8] The verses of C. G. and R. W. before the *Sparagus Garden*, those of Chamberlain before the *Antipodes*, and Tatham's contribution to the *Jovial Crew*.

in such verses, or as indications of the growing tendency of the late drama toward romance in tragedy and comedy. As the great body of Brome's work deals with manners, his most successful vein,[1] the hostile criticism may mean merely this.

Brome's own impression of his place among his contemporaries was, I think, generally speaking, quite correct : a writer of no mean ability, who wrote without illusions as to the value of his work for the future, purely to obtain a livelihood. This practical view he has expressed in the prologue to the *Damoiselle*, which epitomizes him for us :

> *He does not . . . . claime*
> *Lawrell, but Money ; Bayes will buy no Sack,*
> *And Honour fills no belly, cloaths no back.*
> *And therefore you may see his maine intent*
> *Is his own welfare, and your merriment.*

In spite of this materialistic attitude, Brome's works were in greater repute after the Restoration than could be expected from plays written frankly with such an intent. Four of them, at least, were revived, and one held the stage for a hundred and fifty years. The *Antipodes* was seen by Pepys in 1661 ; the *Mad Couple Well Matched* was slightly altered by Mrs. Aphra Behn, and played and published under the title of the *Credulous Cuckold* in 1677 ; the *Northern Lass* was acted in 1684, 1706, 1717, and 1738[2] ; and the *Jovial Crew* three times in 1661,[3] and again in 1705, 1707, and 1708. In 1731 it was made into an opera by the addition of many songs, and continued to be produced.[4] Dodsley,[5] in 1744, gives

---

[1] The *Jovial Crew* is the one notable exception, but even here the interest in humors is strong.

[2] Genest 1. 420 ; 2. 360 ; 2. 601 ; 4. 549.

[3] Pepys' *Diary* for 1661.   [4] Genest 2. 384 ; 2. 395 ; 3. 288.

[5] Dodsley, Vol. 6.

two casts of performances ; Genest adds others of 1760,
1774, and 1791[1] ; and, finally, Charles Lamb reviewed
what I think was probably the last production, in 1819.[2]
Further evidence of Brome's popularity in the eighteenth
century may be seen in the numerous reprints of the two
last-mentioned plays in the Bibliography.

But the public interest in a few of the plays did not
create much interest in the author, for I find but few
personal references to Brome after his death.   One allusion occurs in *Choyce Drollery* (1656), in a satirical piece
called *On the Time Poets*, written in imitation of Suckling's *Session of the Poets*.   The poem begins,

> One night the great Apollo pleased with Ben,
> Made the odd number of the Muses ten,

and continues with allusions to Shakespeare, May, and
others, and satiric hits at Chapman, Dabourn, Ford, etc.,
and finally has :

> Sent by Ben Jonson, as some authors say,
> Broom went before and kindly swept the way.

This old pun, which we have met with often enough
already, seems to have been a hardy perennial, for an
eighteenth-century satirist remarks of William Broome,
Pope's collaborator in the Odyssey :

> Pope came off clean with Homer, but they say
> Broome went before and kindly swept the way.

In 1660, the third edition of Sir Richard Baker's
Chronicle of England appeared, with an added account
of the reign of Charles I.   Here we find the next reference

---

[1] Genest 3. 591–593 ; 6. 148 ; 7. 67.

[2] Lamb's *Works*, ed. E. V. Lucas, 1. 186.   The production, he
says, was a revival after seven years.

---

to Brome, in a list of poets of the age [1] : 'Poetry was never more resplendent, nor never more graced ; wherein *Johnson, Sylvester, Shakespere, Beaumont, Fletcher, Shirley, Broom, Massinger, Cartwrite, Randolph, Cleaveland, Quarles, Carew, Davenant,* and *Sucklin,* not only far excelled their own Countrymen, but the whole world beside.'

Nine years later, Edward Phillips added to the seventeenth edition of *Thesaurus V. Buchleri* of 1669, a treatise on English poets, called *Tractatus de Carmine Dramatico Poetarum etc.*[2] In this, after mentioning Shakespeare, Jonson, and Fletcher, the greatest poets of the age, he continues : ' Ante hos in hoc genere Poeseos apud nos eminuit Nemo. Pauci quidem antea scripserunt, at parum foeliciter ; hos autem tanquam duces itineris plurimi saltem æmulati sunt, inter quos præter Sherleium (proximum a supra memorato Triumviratu), Sucklingium, Randolphium, Davenantium et Carturitium . . . . enumerandi veniunt Ric. Bromeus, Tho. Heivodus, etc.'

References like these last two are scarcely worth noticing, but they show, at least, with what names Brome's was associated. The omission of other contemporaries is significant. Another reference of the same sort is the inclusion of Brome in the catalogue of plays for sale by the publisher, Francis Kirkman. He appended this to John Dancer's *Translation of Nicomede,* 1670. The added title runs : *Together with an exact catalogue of all the English Stage Plays printed till this present year,* 1671. In the *Advertisement to the Reader* (p. 16), Kirkman says[3] : ' First, I begin with Skakespeare, who hath in all written forty-eight. Then Beaumont and Fletcher fifty-two, *Johnson* fifty, *Shirley* thirty-eight, *Heywood* twenty-five,

---

[1] *Shakespeare Allusion-Book,* New Shak. Soc. (1909) 2. 86.
[2] *Ibid.* 2. 160.   [3] *Ibid.* 2. 117.

Middleton and *Rowley* twenty-seven, *Massinger* sixteen, *Chapman* seventeen, *Brome* seventeen, and *D'Avenant* fourteen ; so that these ten have written in all, 304.'[1] I have not been able to find a copy of this list, but I suppose Kirkman includes, beside the fifteen plays wholly by Brome, the *Lancashire Witches* and the *Royal Exchange*, which is merely the *Queen's Exchange* (printed 1657), with a new title-page (printed 1661).

The first criticism of Brome appears in Edward Phillips' later work, *Theatrum Poetarum*, 1675. He says[2] : ' Richard Brome, a servant to Ben Jonson ; a Servant suitable to such a Master, and who, what with his faithful service and the sympathy of his genius, was thought worthy his particular commendation in Verse ; whatever instructions he might have from his Master Johnson, he certainly by his own natural parts improved to a great heighth, and at last became not many parasangues inferior to him in fame by divers noted Comedies.' After giving an incomplete list, Phillips commends especially the *Northern Lass, Jovial Crew*, and the *Sparagus Garden*.

Winstanley's *Lives of the Most Famous English Poets* (1687) adds nothing to Phillips' criticism, but Langbaine's *Account of the English Dramatic Poets* (Oxford, 1691) gives us the first real discussion of the dramatist, and adds many facts about the plays. His criticism is : 'In imitation of his master Mr. Johnson, he studied Men and Humors more than books ; and his genius affecting comedy, his province was more observation than study. His plots were his own, and he forged all his various Characters from the mint of his own experience, and judgment. 'T is not therefore to be expected, that I should be able to trace him, who was so excellent an

[1] A similar list, very detailed, but inaccurate, is appended to Thomas Whincop's *Scanderbeg*, London, 1747.
[2] P. 157.

imitator of his master, that he might truly pass for an original.'

The reputation of Brome since the seventeenth century has been lower, and except for the extravagant estimate of Swinburne,[1] the interest in him has become historic rather than intrinsic.[2]

[1] *Fortnightly* (1892) 57. 504.

[2] An engraved portrait of Brome by T. Cross precedes the title-page of *Five New Plays*, 1653.   The verses under it by Alexander Brome declare it to be very lifelike.   This portrait is reproduced in Pearson's reprint of 1873, in Garnett and Gosse's *Hist. Eng. Lit.* (1903) 3. 9, and in Lamb's *Specimens of the English Dramatic Poets* (Dent and Co., 1903) 2. 246.

CHRONOLOGY OF BROME'S PLAYS

This chronology is merely a condensation of that given in Fleay's *Biographical Chronicle*. In the main Fleay is right, but I have inserted an interrogation point after the dates that I think he has decided upon with insufficient evidence. The dates unmarked are unquestionably correct. Plays enclosed in parentheses are not extant. Facts enclosed in brackets are given solely on Fleay's authority. All others are from title-pages, the Herbert office-book, or the Stationers' Register.

CHRONOLOGY.

Play	Company	Theatre	Date on Title-Page	Stationers' Register	Printed	Fleay's Date
(A Fault in Friendship)	Prince's [King's]	[Red Bull]	—	—	—	1623
New Academy	[King's]	—	—	1640	1658	c1628 ?
City Wit	—	—	—	—	1653	c1629 ? [1]
(Lovesick Maid)	King's	—	—	1653	—	1629
Lovesick Court	—	at Court	—	1640	1658	c1629 ?
Northern Lass	King's	Globe and Blackfriars	—	1632	1632	c1630
Queen's Exchange	King's	Blackfriars	—	—	1657	1631-2
Covent Garden Weeded	[King's]	—	—	1640	1658	1632
Novella	King's	Blackfriars	1632	—	1653	1633
Lancashire Witches	King's	Globe	—	1634	1634	1634
(Apprentice's Prize)	—	—	—	1654	—	c1634
(Life and Death of Sir Martin Skink)	—	—	—	1654	—	c1634
Queen and Concubine	[Revels]	[Salisbury Court]	—	—	1659	c1635 ?
Sparagus Garden	Revels	Salisbury Court	1635	1640	1640	1635
Mad Couple well Matched	—	—	—	—	1653	1636 ?
Antipodes	Queen's	Salisbury Court	1638	1640	1640	1636 ? [2]
English Moor	Queen's	[Salisbury Court]	—	1640	1659	1637
Damoiselle	—	—	—	—	1653	1637-8 ?
Court Begger	[Their Majesties'] [3]	Cockpit	1632	—	1653	1640
Jovial Crew	[Their Majesties'] [3]	Cockpit	1641	1651	1652	1641
(Wit in a Madness)	—	—	—	1640	—	—
(Christianetta)	—	—	—	1640	—	—
(Jewish Gentleman)	—	—	—	1640	—	—

[1] Collier (3. 202, n.) says this was played about 1632, but gives no authority for the statement.

[2] The references in the prologue to the deaths of Jonson and Dekker point to 1637 as the date. This is confirmed by the appended note to the 'Courtious Reader,' which suggests that the play was written for Beeston's Boys, a company formed in February, 1637. Moreover, the reference in the long closing of the theatres on account of the plague (2. 2, p. 260), puts the date as late as October 2, 1637, when the theatres reopened.

[3] By their Majesties' Company Fleay must mean the King and Queen's Young Company, the official title of Beeston's Boys, who occupied the Cockpit, according to Murray (1. 368), from 1637 to 1642.

BIBLIOGRAPHY OF BROME'S WORKS

This bibliography is based on the publications of Lowndes, Corser, Hazlitt, Greg, the Grolier Club, etc., and the catalogues of the British Museum and the Bodleian, as well as the Yale, Harvard, and other important libraries of America. All the facts except the dates of unimportant editions I have verified by examining the various books listed.

MANUSCRIPT

The only manuscript of a play of Brome known to be extant is one of the *English Moor* in the library of Lichfield Cathedral. The Bishop of Stafford, librarian of the Cathedral, has been good enough to inform me that there seems to be nothing of particular importance about the manuscript in the way of marginal notes, etc. I have not had the opportunity to compare it with the printed edition of 1659.

EDITIONS OF PLAYS

THE NORTHERN LASS

The Northern Lasse, a Comedie. As it hath been often Acted with good Applause, at the *Globe* and *Black-Fryers*. By his Majesties Servants. Written by Richard Brome. *Hic totus volo rideat Libellus.* Mart. London : Printed by Aug. Mathevves, and are to be sold by Nicholas Vavasovr, dwelling at the little South dore of St. *Paul's* Church. 1632.
Quarto.

Dedicated to Richard Holford. Prefatory verses by Ben Jonson, F. T. Mag. Art. Oxon., St. Br., John Ford, Tho. Dekker, and F. T.

Other editions:

Lowndes gives 1635 as the date of the second edition, and Hazlitt and Fleay have followed him, but I have found no trace of such an edition in any other bibliographical work, or in any library or bookseller's catalogue.

> Second edition, with sub-title, *A Nest of Fools*, 1663.
>> Other editions, 1684, 1700 ?
>> Sixth edition, with music to the songs by Daniel Purcell, 1706.
>> Eighth edition, 1717.
> Another edition, Dublin : S. Powell for E. Risk, 1726.

THE LATE LANCASHIRE WITCHES

The Late Lancashire Witches. A Well received Comedy lately acted at the *Globe* on the *Bankeside*, by the kings Majesties Actors. Written by Thomas Heywood and Richard Brome. *Aut prodesse solent aut delectam.* London. Printed by *Thomas Harper* for *Benjamin Fisher*, and are to be sold at his shop at the Sign of the *Talbot*, without *Aldersgate.* 1634.

Quarto.

Other editions :

The Poetry of Witchcraft. A reprint of the *Late Lancashire Witches* with Shadwell's *Lancashire Witches and Tegue o'Divelly, the Irish Priest,* by S. O. Halliwell, Esq., 1853. (Eighty copies.)

Reprinted also in *Heywood's Works*, Pearson's edition. London, 1874, Vol. 4.

Selections :

Act 4, scene 1, and Act 1, scene 1, are reprinted in Lamb's *Specimens of the English Dramatic Poets.* 1808. (Ed. Lucas, 4. 101—104).

Translation :

Die Hexen in Lancashire, von Thomas Heywood. Shakespeare's Vorschule III. Herausgegeben von Ludwig Tieck. Leipzig, 1823.

THE SPARAGUS GARDEN

The Sparagus Garden : A Comedie. Acted in the yeare 1635, by the then company of Revels, at *Salisbury Court.* The Author *Richard Brome. Hic totus volo rideat Libellus.* Mart. London : Printed by *J. Okes,* for *Francis Constable*, and are to be sold at his shops in Kings-street at the signe of the Goat and in Westminster-hall. 1640. Quarto.

Dedicated to William, Earl of Newcastle. Prefatory verses by C. G. and R. W.

Selections from Act 1, scene 3 ; Act 2, scene 3 ; and Act 2, scene 5, with various short omissions, are given in Lambs *Specimens,* 1827. (Ed. Lucas, 4. 468—470).

THE ANTIPODES

The Antipodes : A Comedie. Acted in the yeare 1638, by the Queenes Majesties Servants, at *Salisbury* Court in Fleet-street. The Author *Richard Brome. Hic totus volo rideat Libellus.* Mart. London : Printed by *J. Okes,* for *Francis Constable,* and are to be sold at his shops in Kings-street at the sign of the Goat, and in Westminster-hall. 1640. Quarto.

Dedicated to William, Earl of Hertford. Prefatory verses by C. G. and Rob. Chamberlain.

Selections from Act 2, scenes 1 and 2 ; Act 1, scene 6 ; and Act 2, scenes 8 and 9, with various short omissions, are given in Lamb's *Specimens* (Ed. Lucas, 4. 464 - 468).

Act 2, scene 9, reprinted in *English Verse—Dramatic Scenes and Characters*.   Edited by W. J. Linton and R. H. Stoddard.   London, 1884.   p. 193.

A JOVIALL CREW

A Joviall Crew : or the Merry Beggars.   Presented in a Comedy at the Cock-pit in Drury Lane in the yeer 1641. Written by Richard Brome.   Mart. *Hic totus volo rideat Libellus.*   London : Printed by J. Y. for E. D. and N. E. ; and are to be sold at the Gun in *Ivy-Lane.*   1652.

Quarto.

Dedicated to Thomas Stanley.   Prefatory verses by John Hall, J. B., Ja. Shirley, Jo. Tatham, and Alex. Brome.

Other editions :

Second, 1661.   Third, 1684.

Another, with songs and a key to the beggar's cant, 1708.

The Beggars' Chorus, or the Jovial Crew.   1670 ?, 1690 ?, 1700 ? (all folio).

The Jovial Crew, a Comic Opera, as it is acted at the Theatre Royal, by His Majesty's Servants. *With the* Musick *prefixed to each Song.*   London : 1731.   Price 1s. 6d.

Other editions of the opera : 1732, 1760, 1761, 1764, 1767, 1774, 1780, 1781.

A New Book of Songs to the Jovial Crew, 1731.

Airs, Songs and Duettos in the Jovial Crew, selected from the Prompt Book by James Wild.   London, 1792.

The Jovial Crew, reprinted in Dodsley, 1744, 1780, 1825, but not in 1876.   Also in Sir Walter Scott's *Ancient British Drama*, 1810, Vol. 3.

FIVE NEW PLAYS, 1653

Five New Plays, (viz.) The Madd Couple well matcht. Novella. Court Begger. City Wit. Damoiselle. By *Richard Brome*. London, Printed for Humphrey *Moseley, Richard Marriot*, and *Thomas Dring*, and are to be sold at their shops, 1653.

Octavo.

Another title-page :

London, Printed by *J. F.* and are to be sold by J.Sweeting, at his shop at the Angel in Popeshead-Alley.   1654.

Every play except the first is preceded by a separate title-page.   All are dated 1653.   The second and third are ' Printed for *Richard Marriot* and *Thomas Dring* ' ; the last two are ' Printed by *T. R.* for *Richard Marriot*, and *Thomas Dring*.' The volume is preceded by an engraved portrait by T. Cross, with verses underneath by A. B.   There are prefatory verses by Aston Cokayne and Alex. Brome, who is the editor.   There is no dedication. The second title-page of 1654 precedes the copy in the Yale Library.   As the separate title-pages to every play are identical with those of the copies with Humphrey Moseley's title-page, this probably represents a transference of publishers, but not a new edition.   I find no reference to the title-page of the Yale copy in any bibliographical work.   It is not in the British Museum.

THE QUEEN'S EXCHANGE

The Queenes Exchange, a Comedy, Acted with general applause at the Black-Friars by *His* Majesties Servants. Written by Richard Brome. *Regia res amor est.* London, Printed for *Henry Brome*, at the Hand in *Pauls Church-yard*. 1657.

Quarto.

Another title-page :

The Royal Exchange, 1661.   The *Biog. Dram., Dict. Nat. Biog.,* etc., call this another edition of the *Queen's Exchange*, 1657, with a new title, but Brindsley Nicholson (*Notes and Queries*, 7th. Ser. No. 7, p. 126) says that he found by examination of copies in his library that the *Royal Exchange* was undoubtedly the same issue, with the unsold copies prefixed by a new title-page.

FIVE NEW PLAYS, 1659

Five New Playes, viz. The English Moor, or the Mock-Marriage.   The Love-Sick Court, or the Ambitious Politique.   Covent Garden Weeded.   The New Academy, or the New Exchange.   The Queen and Concubine.   By Richard Brome.   London, Printed for *A. Crook* at the Green Dragon in Saint *Paul's* Churchyard, and for H. Brome at the Gunn in Ivy-Lane, 1659. Octavo.

Some copies have ' Five New Playes ' written vertically across the page facing the title.   Prefatory verses by T. S. and Alex. Brome, the editor.   No dedication. Separate title-pages to every play.   The first has two title-pages, one dated 1659, the other 1658 ; the last play is dated 1659 ; the other three 1658.   The first two are paged continuously, the rest have each a separate pagination.

The catalogue of the British Museum lists an edition of 1669, which, I am informed by A. W. K. Miller, Esq., of the Department of Printed Books, is a misprint.

THE DEBAUCHEE

The Debauchee: or the Credulous Cuckold, A Comedy. Acted at his Highness the Duke of York's Theatre. Licensed, Feb. 23, 1676/7 Roger L'Strange.   London : Printed for John Amery, at the Peacock, against St. Dunstan's Church in Fleet-Street.   1677.

Quarto.
An alteration by Mrs. Aphra Behn(?) of the *Mad Couple well Matched* (in *Five New Plays*, 1653).

COLLECTED WORKS

The Dramatic Works of Richard Brome containing fifteen comedies now first collected in three volumes. London. John Pearson. York Street. Covent Garden. 1873. Octavo. With portrait from the edition of 1653. A literal reprint, slightly inaccurate. *Lancashire Witches* omitted.

POEMS

Verses prefixed to Thomas Nabbes's masque, *Microcosmus*, 1637.

Verses prefixed to Thomas Jordan's *Poetical Varieties*, 1637.

Verses prefixed to Shakerley Marmion's *Cupid and Psyche*, 1637.

To John Fletcher [a preface to Fletcher's *Monsieur Thomas*], 1639.

Verses prefixed to John Tatham's *Fancies Theatre*, 1640.

To John Fletcher [prefixed to the folio of Beaumont and Fletcher], 1647.

To Henry, Lord Hastings, son of the Earl of Huntington, [in *Lachrymæ Musarum*], 1649.

Upon Aglaura printed in Folio [in *Musarum Deliciæ* p. 58], 1656.

　　Also in *Five New Plays*, 1659, preceding *Weeding of Covent Garden*, and in Pearson's edition, 1873.

A Song.
'Away with all grief and give us more sack.'
Last two lines quoted in *Jovial Crew*, 1652.

In *Five New Plays*, 1659.

Also in Pearson's edition, 1873.

To my Lord Newcastle, on his Play Called the Variety.
In *Five New Plays*, preceding *Weeding of Covent Garden*,
1659.

Also in Pearson's edition, 1873.

The Old Man's Delight. Three stanzas, signed R. B.,
with two more added by A. B., in *Poems* by Alexander
Brome, 1661.

Hazlitt's attribution to Brome of the verses added
to John Donne's *Poems* (1635) and signed Mr. R. B., is
undoubtedly wrong, for not only is the acquaintance with
Donne most unlikely, but the style of the verses is
totally different from Brome's.

*   *

The Song in the *Jovial Crew*, Act 2, ' Come! Come
away! The spring ' is reprinted in :

J. H.'s *Catch that Catch Can* (with music), 1652.

An Antidote Against Melancholy, 1661.

Walsh's *Catch Club*, c. 1705.

English Verse—Chaucer to Burns. Ed. Linton and
Stoddard, 1883.

Rare Poems of the 16th and 17th Centuries. Ed. W. J.
Linton, 1883.

Lyrics from the Dramatists. Ed. A. H. Bullen, 1889.

Sevententh Century Lyrics. Ed. G. Saintsbury, 1892.

English Lyric Poetry. Ed. F. I. Carpenter, n. d.

The Song in the *Northern Lass*, 2. 6, ' Nor love nor fate
do I accuse,' is reprinted in :

Choice Drollery, 1656.

Westminster Drollery, 1671.   Reprint of 1875.

Lyrics from the Dramatists. Ed. A. H. Bullen, 1889.

Seventeenth Century Lyrics. Ed. G. Saintsbury, 1892.

The Jonson Anthology. Ed. E. Arber, 1899.

*   *

EDITING

Monsieur Thomas, by John Fletcher. T. Harper for J. Waterson, London, Quarto, 1639.

Brome wrote prefatory verses to this volume and dedicated it to Charles Cotton, the Elder.

Lachrymæ Musarum ; the Tears of the Muses ; exprest in Elegies . . . upon the Death of Henry Lord Hastings, etc. Collected and set forth by R. B., London, 1649.

Octavo. Pp. 98.

Second title-page, 1650. Full description in Grolier Club Catalogue, Wither to Prior, p. 94, 1905.

The editorship of this volume is attributed to Brome, I think on good evidence, by the *Bibliotheca Anglo-Poetica* (1815), by Corser, and by the *Grolier Club Catalogue* (1905).

W. C. Ward, in the Mermaid edition of Wycherley (p. 292. n.), attributes the editorship of *Covent Garden Drollery* (1672) to Brome. Besides the fact that this was twenty years after Brome's death, the initials on the title-page are A. B.!

BROME AS A DRAMATIST[1]

The period of Brome's activity as a dramatist extends from the end of his apprenticeship with Jonson, which we may call about 1628, to the closing of the theatres in 1642. The records of his work show that he wrote, or had a hand in, twenty-three plays at least, sixteen of which have come down to us.

In order to determine a little better Brome's position in the history of drama, it may be well to place him with respect to his contemporaries. At the time he began to be prominent as a dramatist, most of the important Elizabethan and Jacobean writers were either dead or had ceased producing. Jonson's popularity had waned, though he wrote three more plays before his death in 1637. The same year Dekker died, but he had stopped writing plays more than ten years before. Fletcher had died in 1625, and Middleton in 1627, before Brome's success may be said to have begun. Heywood, Chapman, and Day still lived on, but were turning out but little dramatic work, the inferior productions of their old age. The only man of importance of the preceding generation who was still active was Massinger, who wrote eight plays between 1628 and the year of his death, 1639. Ford

[1] Since the writing of this section another dissertation on Brome has appeared, *A Study of the Comedies of Richard Brome, especially as Representative of Dramatic Decadence.* by H. F. Allen, University of Michigan, 1912. The main thesis of this study, that Brome is a decadent dramatist, no one has ever disputed, but many of Dr. Allen's points have not sufficient evidence of first-hand investigation to make them convincing. He has not even availed himself of the material Dr. Faust had collected on the very points under discussion. The significant contributions of this study I have quoted in foot-notes.

produced his best work during this period. Shirley, who produced over forty masques and plays between 1625 and 1642, is, I think, the only other strictly contemporary dramatist who is Brome's superior either in the number or the value of his works.

This is not a very proud boast—to be ranked second or third in the third period, the decadent period of Elizabethan drama. Looked at from the contemporary point of view, however, Brome is of more consequence. In this ' brazen age' of drama we call Shirley the last of the Elizabethans with individuality ; Brome we may regard as ranking first among those who succeeded purely by imitation. If we compare him with the very numerous tribe of Caroline imitators, he stands out as a figure of real importance. As a dramatist of humors and manners, he is distinctly the superior of Nabbes, Glapthorne, Marmion, and Davenant, his four principal contemporaries after Shirley. The lesser men who were working in the same field at this period were Jasper Mayne, Arthur Wilson, Sir Aston Cokayne, the Duke of Newcastle, Robert Chamberlayne, William Cartwright, and Alexander Brome. These last mentioned writers, all but one resting in comfortable obscurity, wrote one or two humor-comedies apiece between 1631 and 1640. In the field of romantic drama Brome produced one fine play, the *Jovial Crew*, which had a greater popularity than almost any other play written in the Caroline period. In romantic tragedy he ranks as a merely respectable imitator of Fletcher, not inferior to Cartwright, Carlell, and Suckling.

For a more detailed discussion of the plays technically, a classification will be necessary. Of the sixteen extant plays, one, the *Lancashire Witches*, we may put aside as a reworking of an older comedy of manners by Heywood. Nine more are comedies of manners, with a predominance of Jonsonian humor-characters. These

are the *New Academy or the New Exchange*, the *City Wit
or a Woman wears the Breeches*, the *Northern Lass* (*or a
Nest of Fools*),[1] the *Covent Garden Weeded or a Middlesex
Justice of Peace*, the *Sparagus Garden*, *A Mad Couple well
Matched*, the *Antipodes*, the *Damoiselle or the New Ordinary*, and the *Court Begger*. The *English Moor or the
Mock Marriage* has such a prominent underplot of manners
that it may be classed here, though the main plot is
romantic comedy.   The two other romantic comedies are
the *Novella* and the *Jovial Crew* or *the Merry Beggers*.
The *Novella*, with its Italian setting, is pure romance, but
the *English Moor* and the *Jovial Crew* have English
settings and a number of humor-characters.   Finally,
there are three tragi-comedies, the *Lovesick Court or the
Ambitious Politique*, the *Queen's Exchange*, and the *Queen
and the Concubine*.   These are written in the heroic manner, have some tragic feeling, deal with royal personages,
and end happily.   The scenes are laid respectively in
Thessaly, Saxon England, and Sicily.   Even here, when
Brome is farthest from the manner of Jonson, he introduces humor-characters.

Of all of these plays of Brome, but one seems to have
any problem of authorship connected with it.   This is
the matter of the dual authorship of Heywood and Brome
in the *Lancashire Witches*.[2]   Fleay is undoubtedly correct
in his statement that this is an old play of Heywood's
revised by Brome to make it timely in its contemporary
allusions, for a revival in 1634.[3]   Fleay, however, has
not given a very accurate determination of the parts
attributable to the two authors.

[1] Sub-title first added to edition of 1663.

[2] The five pages following are reprinted from my article, the
Authorship of the Lancashire Witches in *Modern Language Notes* for
this year.

[3] Fleay, *Biog. Chron.* 1. 301.

The evidence which indicates that the play is a revision is in the obvious interpolation of an episode, an omission of one or two incidents that we are led to expect, and a mention in two places of names of witches or spirits inconsistent with the names in the rest of the play. A transaction between Generous and Arthur, involving a mortgage, is mentioned in Act 1 (p. 178),[1] and Robin in Act 3 (p. 210), gives his master Generous a receipt for one hundred pounds, which he has dropped. These two incidents seem to be connected but not very clearly. They also ought to lead up to something, but they are hardly mentioned further. Again, in Act 2 (p. 197), Arthur and Shakstone bet on the speed of their dogs in chasing a hare, but the scene ends abruptly on p. 199 without the interference of witchcraft which we are led to expect. These scenes indicate that something has been omitted in the present version of the play. Moreover, the incident of the boy and the greyhounds (pp. 196, 199–201) is obviously an interpolation with no connection with any of the threads of interest. The boy is brought in again in Act 5 (pp. 241 ff.) as a witness against the witches, but his evidence is quite unnecessary, for the *dénouement* is brought about by the soldier who sleeps in the mill. The final indication of revision is the speech of Mrs. Generous in Act 4 (p. 240) :

Call Meg, and Doll, Tib, Nab, and Iug,

and the use of three of these names, Nab, Jug, and Peg, again in Act 5 (p. 244). The names of the witches throughout the rest of the play are Maud (Hargrave), Meg (Johnson), Gil (Goody Dickison), Mall (Spenser), and Nan Generous ; while the familiars are Suckling, Pug, and Mamilion.[2]

---

[1] Heywood's *Works*, 1873, Vol. 4.

[2] See pp. 187–189, 199–202, 218–222, 235.

The play, then, as published in 1634, is a revision. We may dispose of the possibility of collaboration in the revision by the fact that Heywood was writing for the Queen's Company in 1633, and that the *Lancashire Witches* [1] was brought out by the King's Men, the company for which Brome was writing in 1633 and 1634.

We are able to determine, to a certain extent, the parts that may be ascribed to each author by comparing the play with the three sources that have been discovered. The main plot, the story of a woman of wealth practising witchcraft, finally discovered and condemned, is taken from a celebrated witch-trial in Lancashire in 1612. As ten witches were condemned and executed as the result of the trial, considerable notoriety was given to it. Heywood, with a journalist's instinct, made a play on the subject probably within a year of the trial. [2] Besides this indication of Heywood's authorship of the main plot, the treatment of the erring wife by her husband (Act 4. p. 228) strongly suggests the *Woman Killed with Kindness*.

Closely connected with the main plot are three characters, Arthur, Shakstone, and Bantam,[3] who, in the first scene of the play, accuse Whetstone, a foolish fellow, of being a bastard. At the end of the fourth act, Whetstone has his revenge by showing, with the aid of witchcraft, visions of the fathers of the three gallants—a pedant, a tailor, and a serving-man. Since this incident, as Langbaine pointed out, occurs in Heywood's *Hierarchy of Angels*,[4] which was not published until 1635, and was,

---

[1] See title page to a *Maiden-head well Lost*, 1634, and Schelling's list, *Eliz. Drama* 2. 586.

[2] T. Potts's *Discoverie of Witches in the County of Lancaster*, London, 1613, (reprinted by the Chetham Society, 1845) gives a full account of the trial, but I do not think was the actual source of the play. Heywood probably had merely heard of the trial.

[3] See pp. 176, 189 ff., 246 ff., 250 ff.

[4] Bk. 8. p. 512.

therefore, probably not known to Brome, I assign the parts in which these characters occur to Heywood.

Another interest in the play is the comic situation brought about by the reversal of the relationś of father and son, mother and daughter, and servant and master, as an effect of witchcraft.[1] This part of the play, which includes the characters of Old Seely, his son Gregory, and a friend, Doughty, I can find no good reason for attributing to Brome. On the other hand, as this reversed situation has some bearing on the relation of Arthur and Generous (pp. 178 and 182) in the main plot, it seems to me it must be assigned to Heywood.

The greater part of the rest of the play is taken up with the strange events at the marriage of Lawrence and Parnell, the servants of the Seely family. The witches play all sorts of pranks with the wedding-feast and frighten the guests ; and one of them, Mall Spenser, gives Lawrence a bewitched cod-piece point, which causes a great deal of vulgar comedy by preventing him from consummating his marriage. This plot is involved to such an extent with all the different interests I have mentioned before, that I cannot see any possibility of a separate authorship for it. Arthur, Bantam, Shakstone, Whetstone, Seely, Doughty, and Gregory—characters in the other plots— are present in some capacity at most of the wedding scenes ; Mall Spenser, who gives Lawrence the fatal present, has an intrigue with Robin, the servant who plays such an important part in the Nan Generous plot. Furthermore, there is a piece of external evidence which, I think, indicates that the Lawrence-Parnell plot was in the early version of the play. In Field's *Woman is a Weathercock* (5. 1), one character, addressing another as a very lusty person, says, ' O thou beyond Lawrence of Lancashire.' As Field's play was entered in the

[1] Pp. 179—187.

Stationers' Register Nov. 23, 1611, and the trial in Lancashire, from which Heywood drew his play, was not over until Aug., 1612, Field cannot be referring to Heywood's Lawrence. However, the probability is that both dramatists are using the name of a real character well-known to the audience, or a proverbial name for a person of his type. Whichever be the case, I think it safer to infer that the allusions to Lawrence should be dated as close together as possible. An allusion of this sort twenty years old would probably be forgot. Therefore, this external evidence also points to 1613 as the date of composition of the Lawrence-Parnell plot. Fleay seems to imply that the part of Lawrence and Parnell was added by Brome, because he says that the dialect which they speak is that of the *Northern Lass*.[1] This, however, is not true. The speech of Lawrence and Parnell, which is considered fairly good Lancashire dialect,[2] is much more difficult for the average reader than that of Constance in the *Northern Lass*, who speaks a sort of general North English dialect.[3] As Heywood also has used a northern dialect elsewhere—e. g. in *Edward IV.*—as well as Brome, Fleay's argument is useless.

This attribution leaves very little part in the play to Brome. I think that all that can be shown positively to be his work are the passages that are undoubtedly based on the evidence gathered at the second trial for witchcraft in Lancashire in 1633. These are the short scene of the boy and the greyhounds in Act 2 (pp. 196–197) ; the sequel to it, in which one of the grayhounds turns into Goody Dickison (pp. 199–201) ; the scene of the meeting

---

[1] Fleay, *op. cit.* 1. 303.

[2] Crossley's Intro. *op. cit.* p. 65, n. l.

[3] Compare the words listed from the two plays by Eckhardt, *Die Dialekt- und Ausländertypen des Älteren Englischen Dramas.* 1900, 1. 86 and 87.

of the witches (pp. 218—221)[1] ; and the boy's report of his adventure, at the beginning of Act 5 (pp. 241—244). This assigns to Brome about nine pages in all, out of a play of eighty-nine. Besides this, Brome changed the names of the witches and spirits throughout the play, and probably altered slightly the riming scene in Act 4 (p. 235), to introduce the references to Meg, Mamilion, Dickison, Hargrave, and All Saints' night. He also must have added the prologue and epilogue, and probably the song for Act 2, appended to the play.

All these details of the play, just enumerated, were drawn from the *Examination of Edmund Robinson* and the *Confession of Margaret Johnson.*[2] They must, therefore, because of their later date, have been the additions of Brome. These interpolations have nothing to do with the rest of the play. In fact, Brome's reworking here has resulted in making a worse play out of a very poor one, merely to be up to date.

The authorship of the rest of Brome's work we have no reason to question. Four of the plays appeared during the author's lifetime, apparently under his supervision, for they have prefaces by him, and numerous commendatory verses by his friends. Moreover, the *Antipodes* has an appended note which I think assures us absolutely of its authorship. Ten more plays appeared under the editorship of Alexander Brome the author's close friend. For the authenticity of the *Queen's Exchange* we have only the word of Henry Brome, the bookseller, but internal evidence, I think, confirms this. In fact, in all fifteen plays said to be by Brome alone, I can find no reason

---

[1] The original idea of this scene was probably in the first version, but the getting a feast by pulling at ropes and the presence of the boy, come from the 1633 source.

[2] Both found in Crossley's introduction to T. Potts, *op. cit.,* pp. 59—76.

either in the Stationers' Register, the Herbert Office-
book, or in internal evidence,[1] for doubting the statement
of the title-pages.

STRUCTURE OF THE COMEDIES OF MANNERS

There is a great deal of sameness about the comedies
of Brome, but this is due, not to a lack of variety in types
of plot, as Dr. Faust has suggested,[2] but rather to a
repetition of the stock characters and stock situations
that seem to have pleased Caroline audiences.[3]   Brome's
plots, I think, may be divided into four distinct types.
The *Antipodes* must be put into a class by itself, for but
one-third of it has a regular plot, which is the framework
for the satiric masque with which the rest of the piece
is taken up.   Randolph's *Muses Looking-Glass* is the only
other play I know which approaches this type.

The *City Wit* is a very good play, modeled on the type

---

[1] E. H. Oliphant in ' The Problem of Authorship in Eliz. Drama '
(*Mod. Phil.*, 8. 3), says there are but three plays of Brome on which
we may base a knowledge of his style with anything like absolute
safety,—*Antipodes, Jovial Crew, and Covent Garden Weeded*, and adds
that there are eleven more which may be accepted unless internal
evidence cause us to doubt the external.   He gives no reason for the
particular selection of *Covent Garden Weeded*.   His suggestion that
the *Mad Couple* is probably founded on a play by Rowley, because
it appears on the Cockpit list of 1639 between plays by Rowley
and those of Shirley, I consider ill grounded.

[2] *Op. cit.*, p. 31.

[3] Dr. Allen (*op. cit.*, pp. 44—46) has mentioned Brome's repetition of himself as his most provoking habit.   This is shown in
the repeated types of character (see below p. 64); in the similarity
of the disgrace-situation at the basis of the main plots of *Novella,
Damoiselle,* and *New Academy* ; and in the wearisome frequency
of disguise as a motive in fourteen plays.   ' Secrets of birth, false
marriages, a man marrying one person when he thinks he is marrying
some one else, changed letters, confused identities, timely disappear-
ances, drunken scenes, last scene conversions,—all appear just
as one expects them to.'

of the *Alchemist*, that is, it consists of a series of tricks[1]
rather than of a regularly developed intrigue. Crasy, a
fallen tradesman who discovers that his relations and
friends turn against him when he is in trouble, plots a
revenge upon every one of them in turn by means of a
series of disguises, with the help of his servant Jeremy.
This gives a chance for six or seven excellent situations,
almost any one of which could, like those of the *Alchemist*,
be separated from the others. Some of them, however,
again like those of the *Alchemist*, grow out of one another.
This same sort of duping Brome has used again in the
underplots of two more plays, *Covent Garden Weeded* and
the *Sparagus Garden*. Here we have the fleecing of one
or more country fellows by a band of London scoundrels
or 'roarers.' As I have not come across this 'cony-
catching ' plot in drama before the *Alchemist*, I suppose
we may consider that play the origin of all these scenes
and underplots in Cartwright's *Ordinary*, Marmion's *Fine
Companion*, Nabbes' *Bride*, and Glapthorne's *Hollander*,
as well as those in the two plays of Brome just mentioned.[2]
If these scenes were as typical of the lost plays of the
period as they are of those extant, cony-catching must
have been a stock situation of the late drama.

None of the other plays of Brome can be considered as
merely a series of tricks. The rest of the plots are extremely complicated intrigues. But these I divide again
into two classes, those made up of three, four, or five
interests separable from one another, but united in the
end ; and those in which the various threads of the intrigue are completely involved in one another from the
first act. Of the first class the *Sparagus Garden* is typical.
This has five distinct interests, two of them wholly epi-

---

[1] Woodbridge, *Studies in Jonson's Comedy*, p. 60.
[2] Cf. also Middleton's *Fair Quarrel* 4. 1 and 4, where Chough
is taught to be a ' roarer.'

sodic, the other three brought together into one in Act 5. The main plot is a very complicated intrigue of two lovers separated by the enmity of the father of one and the grandfather of the other. The first underplot deals with the gulling of a country clown. The second underplot concerns the tricking of Sir Arnold Cautious by his nephew and other gallants. The episodic elements are the quarrels of Brittleware, the jealous husband, with his loose wife, and the very realistic tavern-scenes at the doubtful resort known as the Sparagus Garden. The main plot is further complicated by the addition of the unnecessary Moneylacks, father of the heroine, who does much plotting on his own account. The first underplot has one Tom Hoyden, who plots against his brother Tim, the country gull. The second underplot is loosely made to help the main plot by adding motive. There are other minor interrelations all through the play. All those interests, however, are kept practically distinct from one another until the last act. Here they are brought together with some skill. The whole effect of witnessing the play must have been much like trying to watch a five-ring circus with side-shows added !

The other plays that I put in this class are the *Damoiselle*, with three separate interests ; the *New Academy*, with four ; the *English Moor*, with four ; *Court Begger*, with four ; and *Covent Garden Weeded*, with three. Many of these separate interests are extremely involved in themselves—for instance, the main plots of the last two—and have much that is purely episodic besides. The last-mentioned play might be put in a class by itself, because the main plot is wholly dependent upon the exaggerated humor of one of the characters. This makes it exactly of the type of the *Silent Woman*. Just as Morose's exaggerated hatred of noise is the motive at the basis of that play, so Crosswill's desire to act contrary to the wishes of everybody with whom he comes into contact causes all the plotting and counterplotting of his children and friends in *Covent Garden Weeded*. However, as this play has underplots of a long-lost girl turning up and marrying a reclaimed rake, a band of ' roarers ' who gull two victims, and a justice who weeds Covent Garden after much experience with its noxious plants, I class it with the comedies of separate interests, like the *Sparagus Garden*.

The other type of intrigue which Brome has used, that in which the threads of which the plot is composed are inextricably involved in one another from the beginning to the end of the play, has two examples, the *Northern Lass* and the *Mad Couple well Matched*. For an instance of this type I will summarize the situation at the beginning of Act 4 of the *Northern Lass*. Sir Philip Luckless has married the Widow Fitchow, but the pair have quarreled before the consummation of the marriage. Tridewell is in love with Mistress Fitchow, and she with him. Sir Philip is in love with Constance, the Northern Lass, who has gone mad for the love of him. Mistress Fitchow wishes her marriage annulled, but will not allow Sir Philip to marry Constance if she can help it. Constance has two other suitors, Nonsense and Widgine, both strongly backed by different persons who are interested, the Widow Fitchow being the backer of her brother Widgine. Sir Paul Squelch, a justice, the guardian of Constance, wishes her to marry Nonsense. Squelch incidentally has an intrigue with Holdup, a harlot, whom, in order to conceal her, he has disguised as Constance. This is but a bare statement of the situation, without mentioning the episodic scenes and the nine additional characters to help confuse the progress of the plot. The difference between this sort of plot and that of the comedy of the type of the *Sparagus Garden* is at once evident. In the *Mad Couple well Matched* there is the same intricacy of plotting.

Here we have six or seven intrigues, in which everybody attempts somebody else's virtue, though there is not very much virtue in the entire *dramatis personæ*. But every thread is so involved in the others that to take one would necessitate a considerable change in the rest.

This variety of plot is exactly that which became most popular in the comedy of the Restoration. Even when we see it at its highest development in Congreve, it is difficult to follow, and impossible to remembei long. It is interesting to note that both of Brome's comedies of this class were produced during the Restoration period with great success.[1]

The striking characteristic of all Brome's comedies of manners, of whatever type, is the extreme complication of their plots. They are mazes which have to be traversed a second time in order that the reader may be sure of finding his way at any point. To see them on the stage would require such close attention on the part of the audience that witnessing a play would become a serious mental effort, rather than a relaxation. And this complexity is characteristic not only of Brome, but of most of his contemporaries in the field of comedy. Brome has merely outdone them slightly in this respect, and has handled his difficult problem a little better. In Brome, English drama reached an extreme of intricacy which has never been equaled, and never can be surpassed without a hopeless entanglement of the wits of the audience. Even one of the characters in the *Sparagus Garden* exclaims :

> Well here's such a knot now to untie
> As would turn Œdipus his braine awry.

Middleton summed up his own type of comedy in his introduction ' To the Comic Play-Readers, Venery and

[1] See above, p. 30.

Laughter,' of the *Roaring Girl* (1611). Here he compares playmaking to the 'alteration in apparel': 'Now in the time of spruceness, our plays follow the niceness of our garments, single plots, quaint conceits, lecherous jests, dressed up in hanging sleeves.' The comedy of the next generation lost the singleness of plot, and developed the other elements. In comparison with this quotation, we may take one from Richard Flecknoe's *Discourse of the English Stage* (c. 1660)[1] : ' The chief faults of ours are our huddling too much matter together, and making them too long and intricate ; we imagine we never have intrigue enough, till we lose ourselves and Auditors, who shu'd be led in a Maze, but not a Mist ; and through turning and winding wayes, but so still, as they may find their way at last.' Any modern reader will feel that this fits Brome's plays much better than C. G.'s lines before the *Sparagus Garden* :

> Nor is thy Labyrinth confus'd, but wee
> In that disorder, may proportion see.

This last quotation and two more in the plays, may indicate that Brome was adversely criticized in this respect, even by some of his contemporaries. In *Covent Garden Weeded*[2] a character says: 'Nay, mark, I pray you, as I would entreat an Auditory, if now I were a Poet, to mark the Plot, and several points of my play, that they might not say when 'tis done, they understood not this or that, or how such a part came in or went out, because they did not observe the passages.' And again in the *Damoiselle*[3] occurs a similar remark :

> Now *Wat* Observe me :
> As an ingenious Critick would observe
> The first Scene of a Comedy, for feare
> He lose the Plot.

[1] Attached to *Love's Kingdom, a Pastoral Tragicomedy*, 1664. In Hazlitt's *Treatises on the English Drama and Stage.*
[2] 3. 2, p. 50. [3] 3. 1, p. 417.

A thing which adds to the confusion of Brome's plots is his great fondness for introducing episodic scenes and characters.[1]   There is a natural temptation to do this, if one's chief aim is to show manners or humors.   This is the reason for the introduction of the realistic scene of the shoemaker and tailor dunning the gallant in *Covent Garden Weeded*, and the tavern-scenes in the same play and in the *Sparagus Garden*, as well as of the scenes between the humors, Widgine and Anvile, in the *Northern Lass*, and the numerous episodic passages between Courtwit, Swaynwit, and Citwit in the *Court Begger*.   Exact parallels to these are the scenes introducing Dawes and Lafoole in the *Silent Woman*.   Of a less pardonable sort are the episodes which merely add confusion to the plot, without showing humors or manners.   Such are those in which Anvile in the *Northern Lass* is sent to Constance's house, under the impression that it is a brothel, and is beaten ; and Squelch, in the same play, is tried in his own house by another justice, and forced to marry Trainwell to extricate himself from his position.

But in spite of this overloading with episode in some of the plays, I consider Brome a very clever master of plotting.   Of course such involved intrigue cannot be approved of by modern standards ; but if we accept the criteria of Caroline and Restoration taste, we must admit that none of the ' Sons of Ben,' and but few of the Restoration playwrights, equalled Brome in weaving four or five strands of interest into one play.   Schelling[2] and Ward[3] agree in calling him a very skilful handler of plots ; and even Symonds,[4] who has little to say in his favor,

---

[1] Dr. Allen is certainly mistaken in saying that Brome ' chooses his incidents and scenes with a view to 'plot advancement, and, ordinarily, to that alone,' and that ' nothing is shown merely to exhibit or explain characters ' (*op. cit.*, p. 49.)

[2] *Elizabethan Drama* 2. 274.

[3] *Op. cit.*, 3. 131.   [4] *Academy* 5. 304.

admits that his plots are firmly traced, and sustained on one plan throughout, without any suggestion of improvisation. Dr. Faust,[1] on the other hand, says his plays are looser in construction than even *Every Man out of his Humor*, but I do not see how even the most careless reading could lead to this conclusion.

Brome's good points in plotting are his careful exposition in the first act, his attention to motives in the greater number of his plays, and the preparation he never fails to give for any important turn in the plot, except, of course, where he aims at complete surprise. The *City Wit* illustrates these qualities very well. The motives for Crasy's series of plots throughout the play are all carefully elaborated in the first act, where every one of his family and friends goes back on him in trouble. The entrance of Pyannet Sneakup, the shrew, is very well prepared for, so that she comes on in a whirlwind of invective. And near the beginning of the fifth act (p. 358), Crasy clarifies the very complicated situation by recapitulating the part of the scheme he has already planned. This monologue is very useful, and not at all crudely done. This last trait Dr. Koeppel has observed in Brome. He says, in speaking of Massinger's constructive power[2] : ' Same of the dramas of his contemporaries resemble mazes in whose paths both author and spectator may be lost. Richard Brome tried to avoid this by drawing attention to particularly difficult complications by an explicit remark of one of his *dramatis personæ*.'

One reason Brome is difficult to follow, in spite of the craftsmanship displayed in this manner, is that these hints and preparations often come so far before the action that they are forgotten by the audience. Examples of this are to be found in the *Sparagus Garden*, where an important revelation of the fifth act is prepared for by

[1] *Op. cit.*, p. 32.   [2] *Cambridge Hist. Eng. Lit.* 6. 173.

mysterious hints in the sixth scene of the second, and again
in the *Mad Couple*. A place where this preparation of
the audience is successfully accomplished is *Covent Garden
Weeded*. Here a revelation of the fourth act is led up
to by two conversations and a dumb show in the first
three. A very fine dialogue, giving antecedent action
with skilful unobtrusiveness, is that in the *Sparagus
Garden* I. 3. The *Antipodes* is an excellent example of
Brome's attention to details in carrying out his main idea.
Much of the humor of the play depends upon the detailed
consistency in carrying out the inversions of position.
These are but a few of the most striking illustrations of
the playwright's careful endeavor to keep his plots clear.

The plays of Brome's contemporaries, besides having
his weaknesses, are deficient also in his best point—
plotting. Nabbes' *Covent Garden*, for instance, is mostly
aimless dialogue, with little plot, very loosely put together.
Tottenham Court is not much better, and the *Bride* is a
series of separate attempts of a villain upon his cousin,
without any organic unity in the plot. Marmion's
Holland's Leager has another very loose plot—merely
a number of old situations thrown together with but
little sequence. Brome's situations are usually hack-
neyed, but they at least grow organically out of what
precedes. Marmion's *Antiquary* is better, but not equal
to Brome in the handling of complicated intrigue. His
Fine Companion, however, is as good a play as the average
of Brome's. Cartwright's *Ordinary* is devoid of invention,
and absurdly crude in stage-craft. Glapthorne's *Hollander* is clear because it is simple, but his *Wit in a Constable* is most confused and hard to follow, although it has
not nearly so much material as Brome employs in one
plot. Cokayne's *Obstinate Lady* is one of the poorest-
made plays of even this poor period. Beside the four
last mentioned plays, Brome's productions, tiresome as

most of them are, shine like bright metal on a sullen ground. In Mayne's *City Match* we have a plot of some cleverness, but poorly knit and hard to follow. It is a play of complex type, that needs much more care in preparation and explicit reference. Shirley's comedies are not so complex in structure as Brome's, but, though Shirley is superior in most respects as a dramatist, he has often less ingenuity in plotting.

Several times, however, Brome has fallen into a very serious fault in structure. This is the very cheap solution of a situation by the introduction of a *deus ex machina* in the fifth act. In the *Antipodes*, Old Truelock comes in at the end of the play, and relieves us of all doubts as to Lord Letoy's good intentions by explaining that Diana is really Letoy's daughter, who has been brought up from infancy as his own. A quite parallel situation is that of the *dénouement* of the *New Academy*, where it turns out that the chastity of Hannah is proved to her jealous husband by the information that Valentine is her half-brother. Hardyman, her father, is introduced here for the first time to prove this. The *Mad Couple* has two *dei ex machina* in the fifth act. These plays are the only ones in which this inartistic device is used to bring about a real solution. Brome had precedents for this in at least two plays by Jacobean dramatists of the first rank, Massinger's crazily constructed play, *Believe as You List*, and Middleton and Rowley's *Spanish Gipsy*. In the former, two new characters are brought on in the fifth act to solve the situation, and in the latter, a long lost wife and daughter turn up unexpectedly at the end.[1]

---

[1] One other fault, that has been pointed out by Dr. Allen (*op. cit.* p. 51), is that the ' preparation for the last act or the close of it is sometimes inadequate . . . According to long accepted tradition the conclusion of the comedy must be happy,—even the villain must be punished very lighty, if at all . . . So Brome, like many

To conclude this discussion of the structural features of Brome's comedy, his dramatic motives should be mentioned. Three plays, the *Northern Lass*, the *Court Begger*, and *Covent Garden Weeded*, depend wholly upon expectation ; no important surprise occurs. In all the others there is no use of surprise in the first four acts, but in the fifth there is always one surprise, usually in the identity of some character. This method is used several times by Jonson, notably in the *Silent Woman*. The *Damoiselle* has two surprises in the last act, and the *Sparagus Garden* three. Two of these last are prepared for by slight hints early in the play. This cheaper dramatic motive, is one of Brome's weaknesses, resulting from copying Jonson, who used it with real success but once.

CHARACTERS

A perusal of any one of the plays will show that Brome has much more interest in plot itself, in devising and solving intricate situations, than his master, Jonson. He tries to carry out Jonson's principle in characterization, but he never allows his interest in humors to create a play of the type of *Every Man in his Humor* or *Every Man out of his Humor*. In fact, none of the ' Sons of Ben ' attempted anything of the sort. However, Brome does introduce purely episodic humors into his plots.

Brome cared more for humor-study than any other of the Jonsonian imitators, and succeeded best in it. But his humors are nearly all imitations—stock characters of London life repeated over and over in this late period of the drama. Some of these characters portray touches of nature that make them stand out somewhat above their types, and show that Brome was an observer of

of his betters, is prone to convert his villain by main strength in the last scene. For this no preparation is likely to be adequate.'

men, though he lacked the creative impulse to break away from the conventional methods of depicting them.

One of his favorite types is the jealous husband, a perennial figure in drama The four representatives in these plays have nothing distinguishing about them. There are four uninteresting foolish citizens'wives, who are either indiscreet with their husbands' customers or pretend to be. Old knights who are still amorous, and decayed old gentlemen who live by projects or dishonorable employments, abound in the plays. The half-dozen of these, who bear such names as Sir Arnold Cautious and Sir Humphrey Dryground, are rather more disgusting than amusing, with the exception of old Hearty in the *Jovial Crew*. The ' blunt servingman ' is a slightly drawn figure, who occurs in four plays. I imagine Brome's fondness for him may be caused by the fact that he himself was perhaps such a character when he was reading Tacitus to Ben Jonson ; but this is dangerous dallying with surmise. The Puritan,[1] the pedant, and the usurer, figure two or three times each. In his women-characters Brome is quite successful. The shrews, widows, nurse, silly lover of fashion, and foolish mother, as well as the bawd and the plentiful supply of eight harlots, all have an amusing self-assurance and great glibness of tongue. The last mentioned class of women are often drawn as rather pathetic creatures, with much good in them. Besides all these, there are one or two each of the class of ' wenchers,' projectors,[1] a braggart, and a pickpocket. But Brome's best types are the foolish young countryman who comes to town to marry or to be made a gentleman, and is fleeced and made a fool of, the blunt old country gentleman, and the old justice. There are about seven in the first class, and a dozen in the last two. These old men with some special crotchet are the most amusing

[1] See appendix II.

characters of the comedies, but repeated so often that
there is too little variety in them.

In all this array of characters there is little originality.
Not that they are feebly drawn, for there is considerable
vigor in Brome's pen at times, but we have seen people
with these same exaggerated peculiarities from the miracle
plays to Jonson. About the best individual figures are
Mrs. Pyannet Sneakup, a very good caricature of a shrew,
in the *City Wit*; Constance, in the *Northern Lass* ; and
Springlove, in the *Jovial Crew*.[1] The last two are Brome's
only original contributions in the way of character-
drawing to English drama. Constance is a pathetic
figure with a freshness, simplicity, and naturalness that
are markedly contrasted with the rather unwholesome
atmosphere of the most of Brome. She is the only
example in all the comedies, of unsophistication made
charming. Rev. Ronald Bayne suggests that the seventeenth century saw in her some of the charm of the hero-
ines of Scott. The Yorkshire dialect she speaks adds
much to this. Springlove is the best figure in Brome's
best play ; Charles Lamb speaks with some enthusiasm
of him in a review of the play in 1819.[2] Springlove is a
gipsy, whom civilization has been unable to subdue.
The love of the fields and woods and the call of the open
road suggest the late nineteenth-century theme of vaga-
bondia.[3]

---

[1] Walter Baetke (*Kindergestalten bei den Zeitgenossen und Nachfolgern Shakespeare's*, Halle, 1908, pp. 73—76) considers Gonzago
in the *Queen and Concubine* an original type of the child in drama,
a creation of Brome's.

[2] *The Examiner*, July 4, 5, 1819 (*Works*, ed. Lucas, 1. 186).

[3] In connection with this notice of types of character I may
mention Brome's use of dialect and foreign phrases. The *Northern
Lass* contains a great deal of Yorkshire dialect ; the *Lancashire
Witches* considerable fairly accurate Lancashire ; and the *Sparagus
Garden* a little of the ordinary clown-dialect (Somersetshire ?)

REALISM AND ROMANCE

The chief interest in Brome's work to-day as drama is, of course, historic rather than intrinsic, but it also has a real interest to the student of the manners of the seventeenth century. In reading with this interest, one must be careful to remember that the ' realism ' of the comedy with a complicated intrigue becomes almost as artificial and as divorced from actual life as work that is frankly romantic. The exigencies of such plots as Brome is fond of bring about situations that probably occurred as seldom in the life of the seventeenth century as in that of to-day. For instance, the association on the stage of women of character with harlots, a common situation in Brome, probably does not reflect the manners of the age. Likewise, the presence of gentlewomen at taverns was a much rarer thing in life than in Brome's comedies. Artificialities of this sort become dramatic conventions, just as types of characters do.

The student who reads Brome for manners must carefully consider this point. But there are some scenes which are doubtless transcripts of the daily life of England under Charles I. Such scenes are that in which a rabble duck a pandar in the *Damoiselle* (4. 1) ; that in which an old woman is ducked for scolding (in this case, however, a ' manscold ') in the *Antipodes* ; the very realistic tavern-scenes in *Covent Garden Weeded*[1] and the *Sparagus Garden*, and the scenes at an academy of deportment in the *New*

---

so frequently used by the Elizabethan dramatists. Some French and French English occurs in the *Damoiselle*, and one or two German phrases in the *Novella*. (For a complete list of dialect words, etc. see E. Eckhardt, *Die Dialekt- und Ausländertypen des Älteren Englischen Dramas*, Louvain, 1910—11). The *City Wit* has a great deal of Latin, and the *Jovial Crew* several scenes written in beggars' cant.

[1] In 3. 1, an interesting tavern-bill is itemized.

Academy.[1]   At scenes of this sort Brome is very successful.   In fact, the historian of society will find more for
his purpose in Brome than in Jonson, who saw more
humor in universal foibles than in ephemeral conditions.
Realism was Brome's most congenial field, but, like
Shirley, a typical playwright, he tried his hand at whatever was popular.   As romance was in great demand
through the latter half of the period of his activity, he made
several attempts at two or three varieties of romantic
plays.   In the prologue to the *Northern Lass* he says that
he is capable of serious work, and in the prologue to the
Sparagus Garden, actually promises something to ' take
graver judgment.'   This, I suppose, he attempted to
fulfill in the three tragi-comedies.   These Fletcherian
imitations have been moderately praised by Ward,
Schelling, and Rev. Ronald Bayne.   The earliest, the
Lovesick Court, is a mediocre piece of work, but the other
two, the *Queen's Exchange* and the *Queen and the Concubine,* are really interesting, in spite of the fact that
Brome's poetry has no distinction.   All three plays show
the skill in plotting that I have commented on in speaking
of the comedies of manners.
Of the three romantic comedies of intrigue, the *Novella*
is the least interesting.   There is no Jonsonian influence
discernible, but the plot has the intricacy almost always
characteristic of Brome.   In the *English Moor,* a well
constructed main plot, of very good comedy of its type,
is combined with a highly romantic underplot suitable
for a tragi-comedy.   The combination is not happy, but
the plots separated might make two good plays.   The
piece is particularly interesting as an experiment.   Brome,

---

[1] This, again, may be purely an artificial invention.   Shirley,
who has anticipated Brome here in his *Love-Tricks, or the Academy
of Compliments* (1625), may have developed the idea from *Cynthia's
Revels.*

who always affected to despise romance,[1] is here attempting to satisfy the popular demand for it, without giving up his favorite study of humors and manners.

However, in his last play, the *Jovial Crew*, Brome has succeded in combining realism and romance with charming effect.   His method here is to choose an amusing romantic plot, and develop it with humor-characters. The success of the combination is probably due to the fact that the plot itself is a mild satire on the love of romance in young ladies.   With this idea in mind, the situation of the *Spanish Gipsy* is transferred to contemporary English country life, and supplied with humor-characters, which Brome can draw with skill.   The combination of these two forms of art is exactly what Jonson tried in his failure, the *New Inn*.   But Jonson tried to write romance with very little action.   As Dr. Tennant says in his analysis,[2] three-fifths of the play is a bore.   Brome, who is much less interested in satire, or in humor-study for its own sake, and who always has a keen eye for what is dramatic, has been able to avoid Jonson's mistake.

VERSIFICATION

' Each of the Elizabethan and Jacobean men has a metrical method of his own; Ford and Shirley have metrical methods not of their own, being for the most part only those of Jonson or Middleton weakened by toning down to a uniformity of manner ; but Davenant, Suckling, and a whole host of minor Carolans (who, to our comfort, contributed only one or two plays each), have no metre properly so-called of any kind ; they wrote in a system which even Wagner only ventured to hope for, not to act on, of music without bars ; they had no

[1] E. g., the Prologue to the *Jovial Crew*.
[2] *New Inn.*, ed. Tennant, Introduction, p. XXXV.

rule but their individual whim ; and the result was a
hybrid of irregular iambic, certainly not verse, and which
it would be an insult to the ghosts of Milton, Landor, and De
Quincey to call prose.'[1]   This statement of Fleay's, harsh
and sweeping as it is, certainly applies to the versification of Brome.   In fact, the lover of poetry must
read through an arid waste to find a few lines to enjoy
in the work of even the most conspicuous names in the
dramatic literature of the reign of Charles.   Massinger,
interesting as he is as a playwright, has nothing but
facility to recommend his verse.   Symonds allows him
scarcely a dozen lines of intrinsic beauty.[2]

If this is true of the romantic drama of the period, we
may expect to find extremely careless work in the realistic
comedies of manners.   Why these should be wiitten in
verse at all is hard to see.   Yet Brome, following the
custom, wrote six out of the nine plays of this type partly
in verse.   The *Antipodes*, with the exception of a dozen
lines, is wholly in verse.   This rather useless practice,
I suppose, we may attribute to literary convention.

As verse adds very little to comedies of manners, and
in fact, detracts from the realism, we should not be over-
nice in criticizing Brome, Nabbes, and the rest, for their
roughness.   Cartwright, who had fair ability as a versifier,
has shown in his *Ordinary* that long speeches and elaborate
similes in the romantic manner hardly suggest the atmosphere of the dregs of London society.   The more prosaic
the verse, the better it is for this purpose.   Brome,
however, wrote as execrably for tragi-comedy as for his
' low and home-bred subjects.'

In the Prologue to the *Northern Lass* he says :

> Gallants, *and* Friends-spectators, *will yee see*
> *A strain of Wit that is not* Poetry ?

[1] Fleay, *Chron. Hist.*, p. 314.
[2] Massinger's *Works*, Mermaid Series, Introduction, p. XV.

I have Authority for what I say :
For He himself says so that Writ the Play,
Though in the Muses *Garden he can walk ;*
And choicest flowers pluck from every stalk
To deck the Stage ; *and purposeth, hereafter,*
To take your Judgements : now he implores your laughter.

This boast Brome never succeeded in making good, for an analysis of the verse of his three tragi-comedies, in which he evidently expected to take our judgments, shows no more metrical skill than is apparent in the comedies of manners. His verse always averages rather poor, and shows carelessness and lack of ear. Every scene presents difficulties of scansion that frequently make the reader prefer to read the so-called verse as prose rather than take the trouble to determine the author's intention, if indeed, he had any. Lines of no rhythm at all are occasionally introduced, like these two in the *Queen and Concubine* (I. I.) :

> I was i' the' way : but the Queen put me out on't.
> But what of him now in the battail ?

A very irritating rhythm that is a marked mannerism with Brome, is produced by a huddling of unstressed syllables in the middle of an eleven-or twelve-syllable line. For instance, in the first scene of the *Antipodes,* he allows the following :

> Might make a gentleman mad you'll say and him.
> And not so much by bodily physieke (no !)

Another effect that may become very annoying is caused by the jolt at the end of a line with a hovering stress on the tenth and eleventh syllables. For example :

> With an odd Lord in towne, that looks like no Lord.
> Some of your project searchers wait without sir.
> With his old misbeliefe. But still we doubt not.

Another annoying point in Brome's rhythm is the uncertainty as to whether some twelve-syllable lines are Alexandrines, or lines with extra mid-line syllables, or lines with double feminine endings. For instance :

> In competition for the crown as any man.
> For you to rectifie your scrupulous judgement.
> I am an old Courtier I, still true to th' Crown.

Other examples of carelessness in versification are the two ' fourteeners ' in the first scene of the *Lovesick Court*, and the occurrence, four times in Brome's work, of a word divided at the end of a line.[1]

This accusation of general carelessness in technique is not a random generalization based on the verse-writer's early work. I can find no indication of development in skill, no progress of any sort. The examples quoted below, of the best verse I can find in Brome, are both from plays written probably in 1635, the middle period of his production. The late plays, the *Antipodes, Court Begger*, and *Jovial Crew* show no attempts at remedying the faults of the early work. The number of feminine endings and of run-on lines shows some slight variation, but no regular chronological progress. In the use of a certain definite type of verse to introduce variety, the four-stress heroic line, or ' ten-syllable tetrameter,' as Professor Cobb[2] calls it, there is again no evidence of increase or decrease in frequency. While Shakespeare's use of this, varying

---

[1] *Antipodes* 2. 3 ; *New Academy* 4. 1 ; *Queen's Exchange* 1. 1 ; *Weeding Covent Garden*, Prologue.   Shirley is guilty of this in the *Cardinal* 1. 2, and Jonson used it in a few doggerel passages.

[2] C. W. Cobb, ' A Type of Four-Stress Verse in Shakespeare,' *New Shakespeareana* 10. 1—15.   Examples of this type in the *Queen's Exchange* 1. 1 are :

> Betwixt smooth flattery and honest judgements.
> Whom my great wisdom would allot the Queen.

from sixteen to six per cent, makes an added chronological verse-test possible, no such check can be found for Brome, whose use does not vary much from an average of eight per cent.

The model of Brome in his versification I think was Fletcher. The evidence of personal friendship between the two men, and of some influences in details, as well as in the general style of tragi-comedy,[1] makes the theory *a priori* not untenable. Among the distinguishing characteristics of the use of Fletcher given by Fleay[2] are the large number of feminine endings, and the ' abundance of trisyllabic feet, so that his lines have to be felt rather than scanned ; it is almost impossible to tell when Alexandrines are intended.' Both these points are markedly characteristic of Brome's prosody. Professor C. H. Herford[3] has pointed out another distinguishing trait of Fletcher—that ' the pause after two emphatic monosyllables, the first of which bears the verse stress, is common within the line, as well as at the end, and is very rare in Shakespeare.' The use of this in the middle of the line I have not noticed in Brome, but the jolting effect of it at the end, which is a serviceable Beaumont-Fletcher test,[4] is one of the traits which I have tabulated as distinctly a mark of Brome.

The following table summarizes all these metrical peculiarities. It is based on the first hundred lines of six plays of different periods of Brome's work.

---

[1] See above, pp. 20 ; 68.

[2] *Shakespeare Manual*, p. 153.

[3] Eversley edition, *Works of Shakspere* (1904) 7. 154, note 1.

[4] In an examination of a thousand lines of the work that is assigned to Beaumont alone, on external evidence. I have found practically no cases of hovering stress on the tenth and eleventh syllables.

Percentage of

		Weak endings	Weak endings with hovering stress on 10th and 11th syllables	Alexandrines	Four-stress heroic lines	Extrametrical lines with huddling of syllables in the middle	Short lines	Run-on lines
Jovial Crew	1641	44	9	2	7	7	2	33
Court Begger	1640	35	11	2	11	5	1	41
Antipodes	1637	36	10	1	9	9	2	38
Queen and Concubine c.	1635	24	5	2	6	6	3	31
Queen's Exchange .	1631-2	38	6	2	9	8	2	33
Lovesick Court . . . c.	1629	25	8	6	8	8	1	38

After exhibiting Brome's faults as a versifier, it is
only fair to quote a few passages of his best work.   The
following is from the *Sparagus Garden* (3. 5, p. 163) :

> You dare not sir blaspheme the virtuous use
> Of sacred Poetry, nor the fame traduce
> Of Poets, who not alone immortal be,
> But can give others immortality.
> Poets that can men into stars translate,
> And hurle men down under the feet of Fate :
> Twas not *Achilles* sword, but *Homers* pen,
> That made brave *Hector* dye the best of men :
> And if that powerful *Homer* likewise wou'd,
> Hellen had beene a hagge, and *Troy* had stood.
> . . . .
> Poets they are the life and death of things,
> Queens give them honour, for the greatest Kings
> Have bin their subjects.

Brome's best verse is to be found in the *Queen's Exchange*.   The Shakespearian influence shown in situations
and characters may also be felt occasionally in the verse.
I quote two of the most effective passages:

>   At the same place again ?
> If there be place, or I know any thing,
> How is my willingness in search deluded ?

It is the Wood that rings with my complaint,
And mocking Echo makes her merry with it.
Curs'd be thy babling and mayst thou become
A sport for wanton boys in thy fond answers,
Or stay, perhaps it was some gentle Spirit
Hovering i' th' air, that saw his flight to Heaven,
And would direct me thither after him.
Good reason, leave me not, but give me leave
A little to consider nearer home ;
Say his diviner part be taken up
To those celestial joys, where blessed ones
Find their inheritance of immorality.

(2. 3, p. 496.)

Ha ! Do I hear or dream ? is this a sound,
Or is it but my fancy ? 'Tis the music,
The music of the Spheres that do applaud
My purpose of proceeding to the King.
I'l on ; but stay ; how ? What a strange benummednesse
Assails and siezes my exterior parts ?
And what a Chaos of confused thoughts
Does my imagination labour with ?
Till all have wrought themselves into a lump
Of heaviness, that falls upon mine eyes
So ponderously that it bows down my head,
Begins to curb the motion of my tongue,
And lays such weight of dulness on my Senses,
That my weak knees are doubling under me.
There is some charm upon me. Come thou forth
Thou sacred Relique ! suddenly dissolve it.
I sleep with deathlesse [1] ; for if thus I fall,
My vow falls on me, and smites me into Ruine.
But who can stand against the power of Fate?
Though we foreknow repentence comes too late.

(3. 1, p. 504.)

MORAL TONE

The ideas of decency in the seventeenth century were
certainly very different from those of subsequent times.
The numerous contributors to *Jonsonus Virbius* unite

---

[1] A word seems to have dropped out here.

in asserting that Ben Jonson never wrote a word that might offend the chariest sense of modesty.   Ben is always moral, but it would take a bold critic to call him modest. The same thing is true of most of the Jacobeans.   With the Caroline dramatists there was somewhat of a weakening of the moral tone, and a slight increase in the vulgarity and indecency of the dialogue.   But they surely did not have far to go in the last mentioned respect, after *Bartholomew Fair*.   In both morality and indecency Brome reflects the tendency seen in the average plays of the reign of Charles I.[1]

Alexander Brome, in his preface to *Five New Plays* of 1653, is quite right in saying that the plays are ' as innocent of wrong, as full of worth,' but he is not right in the sense in which he intended the line to be understood. Extreme coarseness seems to have become a dramatic convention in the comedy of manners.   Middleton and Nabbes are as great offenders against modern taste as Brome.   Glapthorne and Davenant become equally foul in language, whenever their style is colloquial.   Even the knight, Sir Aston Cokayne, and the clergyman, Jasper Mayne, are quite as degraded.[2]   The dramas of these men reached such a low point that Wycherley and Vanbrugh in the next reign could not descend much further. However, none of them put on the stage such unspeakable grossness as Jonson and Herrick employed in certain of their epigrams.

Though there is no difference in the indecency of language between the writers of the Caroline and those

---

[1] Dekker and Webster's *Northward Ho* is not exactly a moral preachment, either.   The whole atmosphere of it is foul.   Every man tries to cuckold his friend.   Poetic justice is meted out in the end by marrying the worst villain to a prostitute.   In one scene a man is pandar to his wife.

[2] Marmion's comedies are the least open to objection, on this point, of all those of the time.

of the Restoration period, there is some difference in the moral tone of their plots. Plays in which vice is made attractive and virtue ridiculous do occur in Elizabethan drama, but they are rare. The triumph of the rake, Mirabel, in Fletcher's *Wild Goose Chase* (1621), marks the beginning of the moral decline carried on in Shirley's *Brothers* (1626) and *Lady of Pleasure* (1636), and Brome's *Mad Couple well Matched* (c. 1635). In the *Brothers,* Luys is the counterpart of Mirabel, and in the *Lady of Pleasure*, the three gallants, Scentlove, Kickshaw, and Littleworth, are typical Restoration sparks, who talk openly of intrigues, and affect immorality more than they practise it. In the *Mad Couple well Matched* there are four intrigues, and two more suspected ; the bad characters all end happily ; no one suffers for his flagrant immorality ; the hero is faithless, a rake, a scoundrel, and a liar.

This play, however, is unique among Brome's. In all the rest, the good wins in the end. In several of them there is a definite moral, or at least a conscience, in spite of the fact that the aim is chiefly to amuse. An instance is Fabritio's excusing himself to the audience for his conduct toward his father in the matter of the old man's amours.[1] Again we have the highly moral speech of Diana to Letoy, who pretends to tempt her virtue, in the *Antipodes* (5. 2). And in the *Damoiselle* there is a strong moral influence, without any trace of the Restoration manner. In his satire we have perhaps the best proof that Brome worked most of the time with a correct moral standard, for he always, like his master, ridicules folly and vice, but never virtue.[2]

[1] *Novella* 4. 2, p. 160.
[2] See below, Influence of Jonson, p. 91.

SOURCES AND INFLUENCES

Langbaine, who did very creditable work for a pioneer in literary criticism, says of Brome: ' His plots were his own, and he forged all his various Characters from the mint of his own experience, and judgement. Tis not therefore to be expected, that I should be able to trace him, who was so excellent an imitator of his master, that he might truly pass for an original.' This easy way of dismissing the whole matter of literary influence will unfortunately not satisfy the demands of modern scholarship.

There are but two plays for which undoubted sources for the main idea of the plot have been discovered—the *Jovial Crew* and the *Queen and the Concubine*.[1] The *Jovial Crew* has its source, as Dr. Faust has shown,[2] in Middleton and Rowley's *Spanish Gipsy*. He proves that Brome did not go back to the original sources of his story—two novels of Cervantes, *La Gitanilla* and *La Fuerza de la Sangre*—but worked from the English play founded on them.[3] The treatment of this plot shows much originality. The atmosphere, motives, characters, and conclusion are completely changed. The source of the *Queen and Concubine* is followed much more closely. Professor Koeppel discovers this to be Greene's *Penelope's Web*[4] (1587). Brome has enlarged upon the simple

[1] I do not include the *Lancashire Witches*, because the principal share is due to Heywood. See above, pp. 48 ff.

[2] *Op. cit.*, p. 85.

[3] He adds an important suggestion from the *Gipsies Metamorphosed*, and gives a list of six plays in which scenes of the forest and fields occur.

[4] *Quellen und Forschungen* (1897) 82. 209.

plan with additional characters and much romantic decoration, but he has kept not only the kernel of Greene's plot, but also in several places his actual wording.[1]

The sources of the rest of the plays are not so evident as these two. We must content ourselves with possible suggestions or parallels to separate situations. Dr. Faust[2] thinks that the main idea of the *Lovesick Court* comes from Beaumont and Fletcher's *King and No King* (1611). Dr. Ballman[3] puts forth the claims of Chaucer's *Knight's Tale*. By combining the latter suggestion, in the form of the *Two Noble Kinsmen*, with the former, a great many elements of the plot may be traced. I should like to add a third possibility—John Barclay's Latin novel, *Argenis*.[4] There is a resemblance of the conclusion of this with that of the *Lovesick Court*, except that the two lovers are not supposed brothers. In both plots one lover turns out to be the brother of the princess, who marries the other lover. The disappointed man is given the sister of the other as a consolation.[5]

Of the *Queen's Exchange*, no hint of origin has yet been discovered. I have looked for one in vain in the chronicles of Hall, Holinshed, Fabyan, etc. If Brome did not invent this rather interesting and quite intricate plot, he

---

[1] Professor Koeppel shows that scenes 3. 11, 4. 6, and 4. 7 are all independent of the source, but 5. 4 follows the source inconsistently with the other scenes. This indicates that our version of the play was not intended by Brome to be final.

[2] *Op. cit.*, p. 77.

[3] 'Chaucer's Einfluß auf das Englische Drama,' *Anglia* (1901) 25. 54 ff.

[4] Published 1621 ; at least six editions by 1630 ; translated into English 1629, the probable date of the play.

[5] The situation of the *Lovesick Court* is exactly the reverse of that of Shirley's *Changes, or Love in a Maze* and his *Coronation*. If there is any borrowing, the dates show that it must have been on Shirley's part.

probably took the story from some old romance, and
treated it with the same freedom he used with the source
of the *Jovial Crew*. The Saxon names which give the play
a historical suggestion might all be found in Holinshed.
The many Shakespearian parallels in this play I shall
discuss later.[1] Schelling[2] has suggested that the two
stories of which the *Novella* is composed, if not of Italian
origin, at least preserve the atmosphere of the *Palace of
Pleasure*. Hazlitt gives the source of one incident in
this play in his note on Killigrew's *Parson's Wedding*,
which uses one of the same situations.[3] The situation in
which a man, offered an assignation with one woman,
finds a servant has taken her place, is common in Italian
novelists. Hazlitt suggests the eighth story of *Les
Comptes du Monde Aventureux* (Paris 1555 ; a translation
from various Italian sources) as Brome's source here.
The making the servant a negress he thinks original with
Brome, and mentions Casti's tale of *La Celia* as a parallel.

There is no one of the comedies of manners for which we
can prove a definite source for the whole main plot.
However, for the various situations of which they are
composed we can find many hints and parallels. The
discussion of the sources of the *Antipodes*[4] will show in
detail how much originality, and how much suggestion,
is typical of Brome's plots in the plays of this class.
I have not made such a detailed study of all the comedies, but what results I have obtained can be more com-
prehensibly grouped under the headings of the influences
of the three masters in drama whom Brome imitated.

---

[1] Max Koch, in a review of Dr. Faust's thesis (*Eng. Stud.*, 12. 97),
says : ' *The Queen's Exchange* mahnt sehr stark an spanische Werke,
wenn ich auch nicht ein bestimmtes Vorbild nachweisen kann.
[2] *Eliz. Drama* 2. 272.
[3] Dodsley's *Old Plays*, 4th ed., 1875, 14. 480.
[4] See Appendix I.

INFLUENCE OF JONSON

Ben Jonson was the earliest English dramatist who held definite theories about literature. In an age of novelty, his conservative spirit turned to the ancients for his models and his theories. His unusual acquaintance with Greek and Latin literature, and his keen appreciation of the principles at its root, helped him to make a liberal application of these ideas to contemporary conditions.[1] Mr. H. Symmes[2] sums up the result of this as follows: ' Jonson nous donne surtout la méthode pratique. Il rend la composition dramatique possible pour beaucoup d'écrivains. Il donne des modèles et des règles définies. Sa critique est appliquée en même temps qu'elle est théorique.' It is this definite formulation of theory that gives Jonson a school of ' Sons,' while Shakespeare has no special group of followers.

Brome was the most conscientious imitator among all these ' Sons of Ben.' His imitation, however, can hardly be called servile, for it consists in conformity to the master's method and point of view, rather than in a direct imitation of individual scenes and characters. Though I shall mention some exact parallels of both, they are rather the exception. Brome's several attempts at romance, which are by no means his poorest work, show that he was not completely overshadowed by Jonsonian influence.

The relationship between the elder and the younger dramatist was publicly recognized by the one, and repeatedly acknowledged by the other. Jonson's verses, already quoted,[3] prefixed to the *Northern Lass*, show that he was not ashamed of his faithful follower. In the

[1] Schelling, *Ben Jonson and the Classical School*, p. 14.
[2] *Les Débuts de la Critique Dramatique en Angleterre*, p. 169.
[3] *Life*, p. 10.

prologue of the *City Wit,* spoken at a revival, Brome proudly proclaims that

> *it was written, when*
> *It bore just Judgement, and the seal of Ben.*

The highest praise Brome can give to Newcastle's *Variety* is[1] :

> *And all was such, to all who understood,*
> *As Knowing Johnson, swore By God, twas good.*

In speaking of Fletcher,[2] he says :

> I knew him in his strength ; even then when he,
> That was the master of his art and me,
> Most Knowing Jonson, proud to call him son.

The prologue to the *Antipodes* has one more acknowledgment of Jonson on the part of Brome. The relationship was also frequently recognized by contemporaries : for instance, C. G.'s verses before the *Antipodes,* and John Hall's before the *Jovial Crew.* Alexander Brome says he was at first the envy of his master,[3] and later,[4] in defending Richard from detractors, shows that the relationship was quite commonly known.

The discernible influences resulting from this association are : classical tendencies toward the observance of the unities and the arrangement of scenes, suggestions in plot and structure, copied situations, types of humor-character, kind of satire, use of the induction, verbal reminiscences, fondness for learning, and slightly Latinized vocabulary. There are also three direct allusions to Jonson's plays. In the *Sparagus Garden* (2.2, p. 139), ' Subtle and his Lungs ' are mentioned. Cockbrayne,

---

1 Verses in *Five New Plays,* 1659, preceding *Covent Garden Weeded.*
2 Verses prefixed to the folio of 1647.
3 Verses before *Five New Plays,* 1652.
4 Preface to *Five New Plays,* 1659.

the justice, in *Covent Garden Weeded* (i. i, p. 2), says :
' And so as my Reverend Ancestor *Justice Adam Overdoe*,
was wont to say, *In Heavens name and the Kings*, and for
the good of the Commonwealth I will go about it.' In
the *City Wit* (3. i, p. 318), Crack, the boy, says : ' By
Indenture Tripartite, and 't please you, like *Subtle, Doll*,
and *Face*.'

What Jonson stood for in dramatic theory may be
gathered from his remarks in the piologues, inductions,
etc., scattered through his work.[1] He approved not
only of ' ancient forms, but manners of the scene, the
easiness, the propriety, the innocence, and last the doc-
trine.'[2] At first he considered action less important than
words, and words less important than matter,[3] but later
he gave more emphasis to action.[4] Unity of action he
thought necessary,[5] and also that of time, but unity of
place, though desirable, he did not demand.[6] Besides
opposing the romantic tendencies of impossible situations
and lack of unities, Jonson insisted that the drama should
have a moral aim, and that errors and follies should be
the subjects of comedy. The characters should be all
types, the language pure, and the morality should be made
palatable by humor. Finally, poetic justice should be
kept. Very few of these theories Jonson put consistently
into practice, for when dramatic effects could not be
secured by following the theory, he disobeyed his own
rules. For instance, there is often more humor than moral
aim,[7] and often much to violate the unity of action.

Jonson's practice in regard to the minor unities is

[1] The following is condensed from Symmes.
[2] *Volpone*, Dedication.   [3] *Cynthia's Revels*, Prologue.
[4] *Alchemist*, To the Reader, and *Bartholomew Fair*, Induction.
[5] *Magnetic Lady*, Induction.
[6] *Volpone*, Prologue, *Every Man Out*, and *Magnetic Lady*.
[7] Woodbridge, *op. cit.*, p. 28.

consistent with his theories, as far as the circumstances of the age would permit.[1] Brome[2] keeps these unities strictly in but five plays—the *New Academy, Covent Garden Weeded*, the *Novella*, the *Antipodes*, and the *Court Begger*. Four of the plays take place in two weeks or over, and the rest in about two or three days. All the plays, except four with romantic plots, keep the unity of place, interpreted as Jonson interprets it—confining the action to one city.

In another classical practice, which really amounts to a detail in printing, making the entrance of every character a new scene,[3] Brome followed Jonson quite closely in three of the four plays published during his own lifetime. By the time he published the fourth, the *Jovial Crew*, he evidently considered this unnecessary.[4] Nabbes is the only contemporary whom I have observed to imitate Jonson in this point in the printing of comedies.[5]

Artificial points of technique of this kind are of slight consequence. Brome's imitation of Jonson is of a much more fundamental character. I think that even the types of plot he uses are developments of the types used by his master. I have already mentioned, in the discussion

[1] L. S. Friedland, ' Dramatic Unities in England,' *Jour. Eng. and Germ. Phil.* 10. 77—84.

[2] Friedland (p. 85) mentions but one example of Brome's violation of the unities, and considers his allusion to the ' lawes of comedy' (*Sparagus Garden*, Prologue) to refer to the unities. This reference, as well as those in the Epilogue to the *English Moor*, and in Jonson's lines before the *Northern Lass*, I take to mean the laws of humor-comedy or of satiric drama, rather than to the unities.

[3] Jonson speaks of the ' division into acts and scenes according to the Terentian manner ' in the Induction to *Every Man Out*, and follows the principle in the printing of his first folio.

[4] The *Queen and the Concubine*, published after his death, also shows an attempt to keep this practice.

[5] Nabbes also mentions the unity of time in the Epilogue to his *Covent Garden*.

of the structure of the plays, the resemblance of the *City Wit*, and the underplots of the *Sparagus Garden* and *Covent Garden Weeded*, to the *Alchemist*. This type of plot that consists of a series of tricks, a type that became a great favorite on the Caroline stage, I think is the result of imitation of Jonson's great farce.[1] Another result is the fondness for extremely complicated plots. The *Alchemist* has a great many situations, a great variety of trickery, complicated by counterplotting on the part of the dupes, and even by division among the plotters themselves. However, as there is one main interest throughout, the plot remains clear in spite of its extreme intricacy. The lesser men who imitated this could gain this complication only by introducing several interests. The result is such a maze as that in which Brome involves himself in most of his comedies. These many interests divide the attention so much that one may say of many of Brome's plays, as Genest does of *Covent Garden Weeded*, that they have no main plots. Jonson himself, as Miss Woodbridge has pointed out, often has no single line of action dominant, for instance in the *Devil is an Ass*.

Brome's method of exposition of plot and character also shows the influence of Jonson. Jonson almost always announces a new actor before he enters the scene, and very often characterizes the humor of one of his personages in speeches of another. This, of course, is not exclusively a Jonsonian device, but it is carried so far by him that it becomes a mannerism of his comedy. For instance, in *Every Man In* (I. 3), Cob explains Bobadil's character to Matthew, and then adds some facts of the plot in a soliloquy. Again, in 3.2 the humor of Justice Clement is given before his entry on the scene. In *Cynthia's Revels* this method of exposition is carried so far as to become very undramatic. Mercury and Cupid

---

[1] See above, p. 55.

(2. 1) give the character of everybody at such great length that the scene sounds like a long but witty extract from Overbury or Earle.[1]   Brome never carried the method so far as this, but he uses it repeatedly as one of his important technical devices.   Examples are to be found in the *English Moor* (1. 2, p. 9), *Sparagus Garden* (3. 4, p. 159), *Mad Couple well Matched* (3. 1, pp. 41, 44), *Court Begger* (2. 1, pp. 205—7, 213), and *Covent Garden Weeded* (1. 1, p. 3 ; 3. 2, p. 50).   The entrance of nearly every character in the *Antipodes* is prepared for by such a brief introduction.   The use of the soliloquy in clarifying a situation by a recapitulation of certain details, already commented on,[2] is exemplified in the *Damoiselle* (4. 1, p. 437).   The great frequency with which this sort of exposition is employed by both Jonson and Brome—I have merely cited some typical cases—leads me to believe that here we have another direct influence through the study of models.

Influences that can be traced more definitely than those of structure and tricks of technique are the borrowings of situations and scenes.   The parallels with the *Alchemist*, where Kastrill is taught to quarrel and his sister Pliant to be a lady, have been mentioned before.[3]   With the similar situation, that of the bogus academy of deportment in the *New Academy* and the *Damoiselle*, may be compared the news office in the *Staple of News*.   Both establishments are meeting-places for people who are gulled by their own folly and vanity.[4]   These places, and those in which country gulls are taught to become

---

[1] Cf. also Lovel's characterization of Lady Frampul, *New Inn* 1. 5, the epigrammatic characterizations of *Magnetic Lady* 1. 1, the character of Hilts given by Tub, *Tale of a Tub* 1. 1, and the long explanation of Sir Hugh's disguise, 3. 5.

[2] See above, p. 61.   [3] See above, p. 55.

[4] However, see note, p. 68.

gentlemen, are kept by what Schelling[1] calls a group of
' irregular humorists '—a Jonsonian device. The situation of *The Silent Woman*—a man disguised as a girl, con-
cealing his identity even from the audience until the end
of the last act, and bringing about a double climax by
the revelation—Brome has used in the *City Wit*, where
Tryman turns out at the end to be Jeremy, who in disguise
has been helping his master play tricks on everybody
else in the play, though neither his master nor the audience
recognizes him.[2] The reverse of this situation—a girl,
disguised as a man, keeping her identity concealed until
the *dénouement*—which occurs in the *New Inn*, is used by
Brome in the *Damoiselle* and the *Mad Couple well Matched*.
Another disguise, that of the obliging courtezan who is
willing to impersonate any character needed by the scheme
of her employer—e. g. Dol Common's duping of Dapper—
occurs repeatedly in Brome. Dr. Faust[3] has found a
suggestion for the situation in the *Jovial Crew* in a phrase
in the *Gipsies Metamorphosed* : ' Gaze upon . . . this
brave Spark struck out of Flintshire, upon Justice Jug's
Daughter, then sheriff of the county, who running away
with a Kinsman of our captain's, and her father pursuing
her to the marshes,' etc. This passage, however, has to be
wrenched from its absurd context to show any suggestion
of the plot of the *Jovial Crew*.

An interesting parallel in a single short scene is that
between the one in the *English Moor* (1. 2, p. 15), in which
masqued friends enter and make a noisy congratulation
and warning to old Quicksands, who has lately married a
young wife, and that in the *Silent Woman* (2. 1), in which
Truewit does the same thing to Morose under similar
circumstances. Four other parallels in single scenes are

[1] *Eliz. Drama* 2. 287, n.
[2] *Faust, op. cit.*, p. 51.
[3] *Op. cit.*, p. 86.

pointed out by Professor Koeppel.[1] Three of them occur in the *City Wit*, a play which also shows Jonsonian influence strongly in satire and in humor-study. Crasy (2. 1, p. 295), disguising himself as a lame soldier in order to get some money out of Sarpego, is following Brainworm, who plays the same trick in *Every Man in his Humor* 2. 2. In the same play, the scene in which Pyannet gives her husband instructions as to how to behave at court may be compared with *Every Man out of his Humor* 5. 1, and *Cynthia's Revels* 3. 3. Again, in the *City Wit* (3. 1, pp. 309 ff.; 3. 3, pp. 325 ff.)[2] the supposed widow, Tryman, apparently on her deathbed, gives many legacies to the various persons interested, in order to dupe them of their money. There is a slight resemblance between the scenes in which this occurs and the first act of *Volpone*. One more interesting parallel is that between the *New Academy* 2. 1 (pp. 39 ff.) and the *Silent Woman* 3. 2. In both plays an old man thinks he has married a quiet and obedient wife, but finds that she is a virago. These half-dozen resemblances in situation at the bases of plots, and the five in single scenes, need not all be considered as cases of conscious borrowing. Whenever two situations, the elements of which may be identical, are changed in treatment of background, period, or social grade, they often become so different that no one but the student on the scent of literary influences would even suspect a parallel.

The most important part of Brome's imitation is, of course, his humor-study. This becomes patent from even

---

[1] *Ben Jonson's Wirkung, und Andere Studien (Anglistische Forschungen* 20) 120, 134, 151, 154. The first of these is in Faust, *op. cit.,* p. 52. Koeppel is not always careful about acknowledging his debts to his predecessors.

[2] ' *Sparagus Garden* ' (Koeppel, p. 151) is evidently a mistake for ' *City Wit.* ' Also, for ' vol. III.' read ' vol I.'

a superficial reading of a single act chosen at random. This most obvious and easily imitable trait of Jonson's work was most closely copied by Brome, Marmion, Glapthorne, Cokayne, and Cartwright, and to a marked degree by Mayne, Nabbes, and even Shirley and Davenant. However, outside of Jonson himself, there is no such gallery of caricature in English drama as Brome presents.

I have already given a summary of the types to be found in the comedies of manners.[1] In the treatment of all, the manner is most Jonsonian, and in the case of most of them prototypes may be found. The jealous husband, a character of all drama everywhere, need not be considered a Jonsonian imitation. He occurs, however, in exaggerated form in Kitely, Fitzdotterel, and Corvino.[2] The citizen's wife of light reputation, such a favorite with Brome, may be found exemplified in Fallace and Chloe.[3] The idea of the old justice, whom Brome has made the most prominent of his figures, was doubtless suggested by Clement, Overdo, Eitherside, and Preamble. Cockbraine, in *Covent Garden Weeded*, even alludes to Overdo as his ancestor, though the relationship is obvious enough without the acknowledgment. In their interest in ancestry, Letoy, in the *Antipodes*, and Buzzard, in the *English Moor*, show that they are relatives of Sir Amorous La Foole. Of foolish countrymen there are Kastrill and Master Stephen. Tim Hoyden,[4] who goes to London to be made a gentleman, is rather like Sogliardo, who says (*Every Man out of his Humor* I. I): ' Nay, look you, . . . this is my humor now : I have land and money,

---

[1] See above, p. 65.

[2] It is interesting to note that Bassanes, in Ford's *Broken Heart*, and Dariotto, in Chapman's *All Fools*, show as wild exaggerations of this humor in romantic plays as any of Jonson's characters, or even as old Joyless in the *Antipodes*.

[3] See, however, ' Influence of Dekker,' below, p. 106.

[4] *Sparagus Garden* (Faust, *op. cit.*, p. 67).

my friends left me well, and I will be a gentleman whatsoever it cost me.'   The braggart Anvile, in the *Northern
Lass*, is an echo of Bobadil.   Dr. Faust has also mentioned
Captain Driblow, in *Covent Garden Weeded*, as another
descendant.   Brome's blunt servingmen have their prototypes in Humphrey Waspe, Basket Hilts, and Onion.
The clever servant, Jeremy, who helps his master in his
trickery in the *City Wit*, bears some resemblance to
Brainworm and Mosca.   Dol Common I have alluded
to before as the possible original of the many obliging
harlots whom Brome introduces as ready conspirators
in the cause of virtue or of vice.   Finally, we have Abel
Drugger, the city gull ; Sir Moth Interest, the usurer
or ' money-bawd ' ; Dame Pliant, the widow with a
foolish desire to learn fashion ; the Puritans of *Bartholomew Fair* ; and the projectors of the *Devil is an Ass* and
Volpone, all of whom are repeated, though not with
especially servile parallels, in Brome.

   To show further to what an extent Brome carried Jonsonian humor-study, I may mention the *New Academy*,
in which nine characters, practically all in the play
except the two pairs of lovers, are very markedly
exaggerated types.   Moreover, there are a number
of characters throughout the plays which, though
without direct antecedents in Jonson, are drawn strictly
in his manner.   Such are the pedants Geron, in the *Lovesick Court*, and Sarpego, in the *City Wit* [1] ; the three wits
of the court, the city, and the country in the *Court Begger*,
who converse in the same episodic manner as the ' ladies
collegiate ' ; Crosswill, whose eccentricity controls the
plot of *Covent Garden Weeded*, as Morose's does that of the

---

[1] Clove in *Every Man out of his Humor* is, as Faust (*op. cit.*, p. 51)
remarks, the nearest of Jonson's characters to Sarpego, but I do not
think he is an actual prototype.

Silent Woman ; and Pyannet Sneakup, the very amusingly depicted shrew of the *City Wit*.

The use of the humor-phrase as a tag to the speeches of a character—the trick so much employed by Dickens— is not a marked characteristic of Jonson.   In *Bartholomew Fair*, Knockem's fondness for the word ' vapors ' and Troubleall's ' warrant of Justice Overdo,' are examples.[1] The definition Jonson gives of a humor, in the Induction to *Every Man Out*, seems to discountenance the overwork- ing of this rather shallow comic device.   Brome also uses this with great moderation—in fact, not any more frequently than his master.   Saleware's ' Sapientia mea mihi,' and ' Never the sooner for a hasty word,' in the *Mad Couple well Matched*, ' Must we then speak together,' of the Justice in the *Jovial Crew*, and ' Our master is no snail,' the phrase of all the servants in the same play, are the most striking occurrences of the humor- phrase.

In the imitations of structure, scenes, and portrayal of character, Brome has merely gone further than any other of the ' Sons of Ben,' but in imitation of satiric method he is practically the only follower.   Purely satiric passages in the severe manner of the elder dramatist are rare in the works of the others.   In Brome, of course, the satire is merely an echo, without the forceful personality of Jonson.

Though Jonson is essentially a satirist throughout most of his work, he has a definite moral aim in only four plays.[2]   He speaks of making his morality palatable with humor, but, in practice, humor is ordinarily the main purpose with him.   Brome, in imitating him, lashes

---

[1] Nym's ' humors,' in the *Merry Wives*, and two similar manner- isms of speech in *Eastward Hoe* and the *Merry Devil of Edmonton*, are other examples.

[2] Woodbridge, *op. cit.*, pp. 27 ff.

folly, but very seldom vice ; he never has any moral purpose.[1] Humor is his aim always ; satire is merely one means of producing it.   By this change in emphasis Brome has avoided two pitfalls that Jonson's greater love of satire led him into—allegory and personal satire. Jonson disclaims ever making personal references, but *Cynthia's Revels* and the *Poetaster* certainly show that he did.[2] But Brome, in disclaiming all attempt at personalities in the *Antipodes*,[3] is making a statement that holds true for all his extant work.

In the follies and shams he selects to satirize, however, and in the blunt directness of the manner of his satiric passages, Brome follows Jonson closely.   I quote two examples on a favorite theme with both authors :

> Principles to be imprinted in the heart of every new made gentleman : To commend none but himselfe : to like no mans wit but his owne : to slight that which he understands not : to lend mony and never look for't agen : to take up upon obligation, and lend out upon affection : to owe much, but pay little : to sell land but buy none : to pawn, but never to redeem agen : to fight for a whore : to cherish a Bawd, and defie a tradesman.
> (*Sparagus Garden* 4. 9, p. 194)

> Ile tell you a briefe character was taught me. Speake nothing that you mean, performe nothing that you promise, pay nothing that you owe, flatter all above you, scorne all beneath you, deprave all in private, praise all in publike ; keep no truth in your mouth, no faith in your heart ; no health in your bones, no friendship in your mind, no modesty in your eyes, no Religion in your conscience ; but especially no Money on your Purse.
> (*City Wit* 3. 2, p. 306.)

Though I can find no verbal parallel to these passages in Jonson, the general tone of them, and many of the ideas,

---

[1] The dupes in the *City Wit* are tricked because of their dishonesty, and virtue presides over the solution, but the aim of the play is purely comic.

[2] Woodbridge, p. 33.   [3] 2. 5, p. 265.

are to be found in the satiric dialogue in the first part of the first scene of *Every Man Out*.[1]

The following passage on the origin of fashions has also a certain Jonsonian bluntness, though here again there is no direct parallel :

> I am for the naked Neck and Shoulders, then.
> For (I tell you Mistress) I have a white Skin,
> And a round straight Neck ; smooth and plump Shoulders,
> Free from French Flea-bits, and never a wrinckle
> Neare 'em though I say't.
>
> 'T has been suggested by invective men,
> Women to justifie themselves that way.
> Began that fashion. As one tother side,
> The fashion of mens Brow-locks was perhaps
> Devis'd out of necessity, to hide
> An il-graced forehead ; Or besprinkled with
> The outward Symptoms of some inward griefe.
> As, formerly the Saffron-steeped Linnen,
> By some great man found usefull against Vermine,
> Was ta'ne up for fashionable wearing.
> Some lord that was no Niggard of his Beauty,
> Might bring up narrow brims to publish it.
> Another to obscure his, or perhaps
> To hide defects thereof, might bring up broad ones,
> As questionless, the straight, neat timbered leg,
> First wore the Troncks, and long Silk-hose ; As likely
> The Baker-knees, or some strange shamble shanks
> Begat the Ancle breeches.   (*Damoiselle* 5. 1, p. 456.)

The dialogue in which this passage occurs also has some hits at woman's affectations and face-painting—themes which Jonson never tires of.   The same thing is referred to in the *City Wit* (2. 2, p. 300), where Crasy, disguised as a doctor, says : ' As for Gellies, Dentifrices, Diets, Mineral Fucusses, Pomatums, Fumes, Italian Masks to

---

[1] Cf. also Marmion's reminiscence of the same passage in *Holland's Leager* 2. 5, p. 41.

sleep in, either to moisten or dry the superficies of your face,' etc. I have suggested elsewhere that the absurdly stilted language of courtship and compliment used in the academy of ' French carriage ' in the *New Academy* (4. 2, p. 79), as well as the same thing in the *Antipodes* (4. 6, 7, 8) and the *Sparagus Garden* (4. 9, 10, pp. 195 ff.), may be a reminiscence of the language of courtship which Amorphus teaches Asotus in *Cynthia's Revels.* Other passages, Jonsonian in style, though not imitations, are the remarks on the qualities of a good servant in the *Northern Lass* (4. 1, pp. 69—71), and that on the disadvantages of honesty and the ways of London tradesmen, in the *City Wit* (1. 1, p. 284), quoted by Faust, Ward, and Bayne. Dr. H. S. Murch[1] has called attention to the ridicule in *Covent Garden Weeded* (2. 1, p. 23) of the reading of old-fashioned romances. The influence of Jonson in the satire on the Puritans, lawyers, and projectors is discussed later in Appendix II. A typical play to read for the Jonsonian harshness of touch in satire is the early piece, the *Northern Lass.*

The display of learning that is so marked in Jonson can hardly be called a trait of Brome. Schelling, in speaking of Nabbes,[2] says that he is free from pedantry and fine writing, darling sins of most of the sons of Ben. Brome should also be included in the exception. Such a scene as 4. 4 of *Staple of News*, with its allusions to heraldry, anatomy, astrology, geometry, prosody, and law, was quite impossible for Brome to imitate, not because he knew better, but because he did not know enough. In the prologue to the *Novella* he contemptuously refers his hearers who look for more than ' Mirth and Sence ' to

Those Poet-Bownces that write English Greeke.

[1] *Knight of the Burning Pestle (Yale Studies in English. 33. lxxiii).*
[2] *Eliz. Drama 2. 281.*

Once in a while, however, he has a passage that suggests
an attempt to display some out of the way facts, showing
that his contempt was due to lack of knowledge rather
than to good judgment. For instance, the speeches of
the Jonsonian figure, Sarpego, the pedant in the *City
Wit*, bristle with Latin phrases and classical allusions,
but none of them show special erudition. In the *Sparagus
Garden* (2. 1, p. 136) there is a long list of aphrodisiacs.
Ward[1] suggests three other similar examples—the vaga-
bond's argot in the *Jovial Crew*, the military terms in
Covent Garden Weeded (5. 3), and the enumeration of
dances in the *New Academy* (3. 2). But all this learning,
if it may be called so, culled from three volumes of plays,
is not so much as Jonson has put into the single scene
mentioned above. A comparison of any act in Brome's
plays with one of Marmion's will show a marked difference
in pedantic affectation and fine writing.

There is an affectation, however, that Brome has
acquired from the imitation of his master—that of a
fondness for unusual words, particularly for words of
Latin derivation. Schelling[2] cites some of Jonson's
Latinisms of phrase and word, but says that his vocabulary is remarkably English for a scholar of his day.
I think, however, his vocabulary is a little heavier than
that of most of the comic dramatists. He speaks in one
place of a character who is ' like one of your ignorant
poetasters of the time, who, when they have got acquainted with a strange word, never rest till they have wrung
it in, though it loosen the whole fabric of the sense.'[3]
Again, in the *Poetaster*, he ridicules Marston for the use
of such words as *oblatrant, furibund, fatuate,* and *strenuous.*
These words sound very like some of Brome's attempts
at the unusual. In the *Lovesick Court* occur *morigerous,*

---

[1] *Dict. Nat. Biog.* 6. 395.
[2] Jonson's *Timber*, Introduction, p. xxii.   [3] *Cynthia's Revels* 2. 1.

oraculous perduit, testudinous, auspicate, æquability, procere
(used of grass), and *induce* (applied to a masque ; cf.
Jonson's *induce a morris,* used in the *Satyr*). In the
City Wit we find *deprome, suspiration, surphuled, car-
kanetted, outrecuidance. Covent Garden Weeded* has *dehort,*
and *Sparagus Garden, depusilated.* In the *Antipodes*
occur *somniferous, capital* (used of a beaver hat), and
lacerate (used of papers). Some of these words I quote,
not because they are unusual in themselves, but because
they sound very pedantic in their context. Not many
of them have actual precedents in Jonson's usage, but
I think his style would easily lead an inferior mind like
Brome's into the pitfall of verbal pedantry.

Actual verbal reminiscences of Jonson are not so
common as might be expected. Dr. Faust has noted
one in the *City Wit.*[1] Sarpego says : ' Diogenes Laertius
on a certain time demanded of Cornelius Tacitus, an
areopagite of Syracusa, what was the most commodious
and expeditest method to kill the itch.' This may be
compared with Clove's speech in *Every Man Out* :
' Aristotle in his dæmonologia approves Scaliger for the
best navigator in his time, and in his hypercritics he re-
ports him to be Heautontimorumenos ' ! Another parallel noted by Dr. Faust[2] occurs in the *Antipodes* (1. 5,
p. 244) : Blaze tells Letoy that the herald has Letoy's
genealogy

> Full four descents beyond
> The conquest, my good Lord, and finds that one
> Of your French ancestry came in with the Conqueror.
> Letoy : Iefrey Letoy, twas he, from whom the English
> Letoys have our descent.

La-Foole in the Silent Woman (1. 4) says :

> They all come of our house, the La-Fooles of the north, the
> La-Fooles of the west, the La-Fooles of the south—we are as

---

[1] Faust, *op. cit.,* p. 52.   [2] *Op. cit.,* p. 59.

ancient a family as any in England, but I myself am descended lineally of the French La-Fooles.

Ward[1] points out another passage in Brome, parallel to this in the *English Moor* (3. 2, p. 43) : ' The Buzzards are all gentlemen. We came in with the Conqueror. Our name (as the French has it) is Beaudesert.' Two more verbal reminiscences have been noted by Professor Koeppel.[2] The same Malapropism which occurs in *Covent Garden Weeded* (1. 1, p. 10), where, after a song one character says, ' O most melodious,' and another, ' Most odious, Did you say ? It is methinks most odoriferous,' is to be found in the *Poetaster* (4. 1), where, after Crispinus sings, Albius remarks, ' O, most odoriferous music ! ' The general resemblance of *Covent Garden Weeded* 1. 1 and *Alchemist* 4. 2 has already been noted. There is also a verbal resemblance in Clotpoll's speech (p. 11), ' Do you think if I give my endeavor to it, I shall ever learn to roar and carry it as you do, that have it naturally as you say ' ? and Kastrill's ' Do you think doctor, I e'er shall quarrel well ' ?

One last detail in which Brome imitated Jonson is a minor one, but obvious. This is the use of the ' induction.' With Brome we never find it in such elaborate form as those of *Bartholomew Fair*, *Every Man out of his Humor*, or the *Staple of News*, but it appears rather as a humorous and somewhat longer prologue than usual. The *City Wit* has one of this sort spoken by the pedant in the play, and the prologue to the *Novella* has a humorously impromptu air that suggests Jonson. The long epilogue to the *Court Begger*, with its personal remarks and advertisement of the author's works, is another example of the same kind of thing. Another similar and purely external device is that of occasionally adding a brief characterization of

---

[1] *Op. cit.*, 3. 129, n. 2.   [2] *Op. cit.*, pp. 145, 169.

some of the *dramatis personæ* in printing a play. For instance, before the *Mad Couple well Matched*, we read ' Wat, a blunt fellow,' ' Mrs. Crostill, a rich Vintners Widow, and humorous ' ; before the *Court Begger*, ' Mr. Courtwit, a Complimenter,' ' Mr. Swaynwit, a blunt Country Gentleman,' ' Mr. Citwit, a citizens son that supposes himself a wit,' ' Sir Raphael, an old Knight that talkes much and would be thought wise,' etc. This is a very faint imitation of the long character-sketches that precede the early plays of Jonson.

After all this detailed discussion of the influence of Jonson on Brome, I repeat what I said at the beginning of it, that Brome's imitation is not a completely servile copying. His plays are the work of a man who learned playwriting by being apprenticed to it as a trade, just as he might have learned carpentry. He followed his master's methods, and applied them to his own pieces of work with much skill and intelligence, but without much literal plagiarism and without any originality.

INFLUENCE OF SHAKESPEARE

The influence of Shakespeare on Brome has naturally been worked out with much care. Certain of the more obvious indications of it have been pointed out by Ward and by Dr. Faust, but a full study of the question is to be found in Professor Koeppel's *Studien über Shakespeare's Wirkung auf Zeitgenössische Dramatiker*.[1] This careful work must be supplemented, however, by a few further cases of resemblance.

Professor Koeppel says, in introducing his chapter on Brome : ' In verschwenderischer weise hat Richard Brome die stoffe verwendet, die ihm das drama und die

[1] *Materialien zur Kunde des Älteren Englischen Dramas* (1905) **9. 42—47.**

prosa seiner vorgänger und zeitgenossen boten. Er
nimmt sich dabei selten die zeit, ein motiv sauber heraus-
zuarbeiten und es organisch mit der haupthandlung zu
verknüpfen; er will nur durch eine möglichst bunte
reihenfolge von scenen fesseln. Begreiflicher weise
werden wir in dem sammelsurium seiner production oft
auch an Shakespeare erinnert — Bromes freundschaft
mit Ben Jonson, der als dichter in erster linie sein vorbild war, hielt ihn nicht ab, auch die werke des grossen
dichterischen antipoden seines meisters für seine zwecke
auszubeuten.'

But once does Brome refer to Shakespeare by name.
In the *Antipodes*,[1] Letoy says of his troop of actors,

> These lads can act the Emperors lives all over,
> And Shakespeares Chronicled histories to boot.'

But there are, besides this passage, many cases of
parallelism which show an undoubted knowledge of
Shakespeare.

Of the several resemblances in situations, most are too
slight to prove any direct influence. There is a rather
unimportant resemblance between the situation in one
of the minor interests in the *Mad Couple well Matched*—
in which Alicia, the light wife of the merchant Saleware,
falls in love with Bellamy, a woman in disguise—and the
Olivia-Viola motive in *Twelfth Night*. Professor Koeppel's
comment on this is [2] : ' Schon diese andeutungen genügen,
uns erkennen zu lassen, dass sich Brome's *dramatis personæ*
in einer viel unreineren luft bewegen als Shakespeare's
gestalten ' ; but I think the resemblance too slight to
suggest anything else. The same monograph has a comparison of the main outline of the *City Wit* with *Timon
of Athens*.[3] Here, again, I should say that the **resem-**
blance is too slight to be worth noting, were it not for a

---

[1] 1. 5.   [2] *Op. cit.*, p. 43.   [3] *Op. cit.*, p. 43.

rather close verbal imitation of a single passage. There is no likeness in plot or chaiacter, but merely in the situation of a man refused credit by his friends when he has suffered financial reverses. The attitude of mind and the behavior of the leading character in the two plays are totally different. A much more obvious case of borrowing is that pointed out by Professor Koeppel[1] between the *Court Begger*, Act 3, and the *Merchant of Venice* I. 2. Lady Strangelove and her maid Philomel discuss the lady's lovers with great freedom, much as Portia and Nerissa discuss Portia's.

The *Queen's Exchange* is much more reminiscent of Shakespeare than any other of Brome's plays. Professor Koeppel,[2] following Ward's hint,[3] has shown the resemblance of the relations between Segebert and his sons, Anthynus and Offa, to those of Lear and his daughters, as well as a further parallel between the two sons and Edgar and Edmund in *Lear*. Another instance of indebtedness in the same play is the fact that Anthynus has a vision, in which six West-Saxon kings appear in dumb show,[4] like the show of Scottish kings in *Macbeth*. Dr. Faust[5] finds a resemblance between the scene in which Segebert and Anthynus are set upon by Offa and that in *Macbeth* in which Banquo is murdered and Fleance escapes, but I doubt whether any one else can detect any similarity. Dr. Faust has two better suggestions, however—the comparison of the flight of the lovers in the *Novella* with the elopement of Lorenzo and Jessica in the *Merchant of Venice*,[6] and the parallel between Victoria's characterization of her lovers in the same play and the dialogue between Portia and Nerissa,[7] which Brome borrowed again in the *Court Begger*. Furthermore,

---

[1] *Op. cit.*, p. 44.   [2] *Op. cit.*, p. 46.   [3] Ward, *op. cit.*, 3. 129, n. 4.
[4] Act 3. p. 505.   [5] Faust, *op. cit*, p. 94.
[6] Faust, *op. cit.*, p. 80.   [7] Faust, *op. cit.*, p. 80.

there is a passage in *Antipodes* 2. 2 that is an undoubted
imitation of Hamlet's advice to the players in *Hamlet*
3. 2.[1] To these examples may be added one more. The
scene in the *City Wit* (3. 2), in which Pyannet assumes
the part of the prince, so that her husband may practise
bargaining the sale of his jewels, may be compared with
the famous one in which Falstaff takes the part of the
king (1 *Hen. IV.* 2. 4).

Brome seems to have been indebted to Shakespeare
also for a half dozen of his characters.   Garrula, in the
Lovesick Court, is one of the numerous imitations of the
Nurse in *Romeo and Juliet*.   The likeness is especially
close in Act 1, scene 2 (p. 98); cf. *Romeo and Juliet* 2. 5.[2]
Swinburne suggests another imitation of Juliet's nurse
in Closet, ' an old Crone, Nurse-keeper,' in a *Mad Couple
well Matched*.[3]   In the same play, the ' Methodicall,
Grave, and Orthographicall speaking friend Mr. Saveall,
that cals People Pe-o-ple '[4] seems to be a faint reminiscence of Holofernes,[5] but the resemblance is more in this
description than in the later working out of the character
himself.   Andrea, the faithful fool, in the *Queen and
Concubine*, who follows his mistress into exile, is very like
the Fool in *Lear* ; the parson with his scraps of Latin
is another repetition of Holofernes ; and the misuse of
words by Lollio and Poggio suggests Dogberry and
Verges.[6]

There are, moreover, three or four verbal reminiscences of Shakespeare in Brome. The parallel passages
from the *City Wit* and *Timon of Athens*, alluded to before,
are as follows :

'All things rob another : Churches poule the People,
Prices pill the Church ; Minions draw from Princes,

[1] Quoted in Appendix I.   [2] Koeppel, *op. cit.*, p. 45.
[3] *Fortnightly* 57. 502.   [4] *Mad Couple well Matched* 1. 1, p. 5.
[5] Koeppel, *op. cit.*, p. 42.   [6] Koeppel, *op. cit.*, p. 47.

Mistresses suck Minions, and the Pox undoes Mistresses ;
Physicians plague their Patients ; Orators their Clients ;
Courtiers their Suitors, and the Devill all.   The water
robs the earth, earth choakes the water : fire burns ayre,
ayre still consumes the fire.

> Since Elements themselves do rob each other,
> And *Phoebe* for her light doth rob her brother,
> What ist in man, one man to rob another.'
>
> *(City Wit* 4. 1. p. 341.)

>   I'll example you with thievery :
> The sun's a thief, and with his great attraction
> Robs the vast sea : the moon's an arrant thief,
> And her pale fire she snatches from the sun :
> The sea's a thief, whose liquid surge resolves
> The moon into salt tears ; the earth's a thief,
> That feeds and breeds by a composture stolen
> From general excrement ; each thing's a thief :
> The laws, your curb and whip, in their rough power
> Have uncheck'd theft.   Love not yourselves : away,
> Rob one another.
>
> *(Timon of Athens* 4. 3, 438 ff.)

A simile in the *English Moor* may be compared with
one in I *Henry IV* :

>   This alters not thy beauty,
> Though for a time obscures it from our eyes.
> Thou maist be, while at pleasure, like the Sun ;
> Thou dost but case thy splendour in a cloud,
> To make the beam more precious in[1] it shines.
> In stormy troubled weather no Sun's seen. . . .
> But let the roaring tempest once be over,
> Shine out again and spare not.
>
> *(English Moor* 3. I, p. 38.)

> Yet herein will I imitate the sun,
> Who doth permit the base contagious clouds

---

[1] ' when ' ?

> To smother up his beauty from the world,
> That, when he please again to be himself,
> Being wanted, he may more be wondered at,
> By breaking through the foul and ugly mists
> Of vapours that did seem to strangle him.
>
> (1 *Henry IV.* 1. 2, 221 ff.)

These two parallels have been discovered by Professor Koeppel. Dr. Faust[1] compares the opening lines of the *Queen and Concubine,*

> The clouds of Doubts and Fears are now dispers'd,
> And Joy, like the resplendent Sun spreads forth
> New life and spirit over all this Kingdom
> That lately gasp'd with Sorrow,

with the beginning of *Richard III.*

> Now is the winter of our discontent
> Made glorious summer by this sun of York ;
> And all the clouds, that lower'd upon our house,
> In the deep bosom of the ocean buried.

I should like to add one more verbal reminiscence from the prologue to the *Damoiselle :*

> Bayes will buy no Sack,
> And Honour fills no belly, cloaths no back.

This is an echo of Falstaff's soliloquy on the same subject (1 *Henry IV.* 5. 1).

In general, the influence of Shakespeare on Brome differs from that of Jonson in that it consists wholly of details, rather than of principles or point of view. Whether many of these details are genuine cases of influence I am extremely doubtful.

---

[1] *Op. cit.,* p. 100.

INFLUENCE OF DEKKER

Prefixed to the first edition of the *Northern Lass,* Brome's first publication (1632), are the following lines :

> To my Sonne Broom and his Lasse.
> *Which, then of Both shall I commend ?*
> *Or thee (that art my Son and Friend)*
> *Or Her, by thee begot ? A Girle*
> *Twice worth the* Cleopatrian *Pearl.*
> *No, 'tis not fit for me to Grace*
> *Thee, who art mine ; and to thy Face.*
>   *Yet I could say, the merriest* Maid
> *Among the* Nine, *for thee has laid*
> *A Ghyrland by ; and jeers to see*
> *Pyed Ideots fear the* Daphnean *Tree ;*
> *Putting their eyes out with those* Boughs
> *With which she bids me deck thy Brows.*
>   *But what I bring shall crown thy* Daughter
> *(My* Grand-child) *who (though full of laughter)*
> Is chaste and witty to the time ;
> *Not lumpish-cold, as is her Clime.*
> *By* Phoebus *Lyre, thy* Northern Lasse
> *Our Southern proudest Beauties passe :*
>   Be Jovial *with thy Brains (her Mother)*
> *And help her* (Dick) *to such another.*
>   Tho. Dekker.

The presence of these verses, with such an intimate title of address, doubtless gave the hint to Fleay that Brome may have been influenced by Dekker. He does not say what this consists in, but merely says it is apparent in the *City Wit*.[1] Schelling mentions that Dekker ' appears to have imparted some of his easy humor, although no scruple of Dekker's subtler gift, that of poetry, is discoverable in the verses of Brome.'[2] Bayne even goes so far as to say that Brome ' is more truly a ' son ' of Dekker than of Jonson. His best and happiest

[1] Fleay, *Biog. Chron.*, 1. 36.   [2] Schelling, *Eliz. Drama* 2. 269.

work is in the vein of Dekker.' He attributes the gaiety and lightness of touch of parts of Brome to this influence.[1]

But all this is very vague, and easily overestimated. I doubt whether we should have heard so much of the influence of Dekker had he not written the prefatory verses quoted above. However, if we may safely attribute to Dekker the occasional un-Jonsonian touches of idealism or of pathos that we find in Brome, there are a few that are worth pointing out. In the *Northern Lass* (4. 3, p. 75), Constance Holdup, a harlot, laments the wretched condition of her class in a way that is strongly reminiscent of the *Honest Whore,*[2] though there is no verbal parallel. Another bit of pathos, the most effective in all the plays, is the scene in the *Damoiselle*[3] in which Phillis, ' a poore Wench,' talks of her mother and her lost father. This is the sort of thing that Jonson's harsher nature never attempted. The first two scenes of the *Sparagus Garden* have the easy humor that Schelling mentions, and some of the finer imagination of Dekker in the passages in praise of love and poetry. This sort of thing, as Bayne says, makes a strange contrast with the rough Jonsonian manner and crass realism of the greater part of Brome.[4]

It is a curious fact that the part of Dekker's work that shows most definitely in Brome is his worst. *Northward Ho* and *Westward Ho*, by Dekker and Webster, are the two plays that are most like Brome's, and that represent the lowest depths of grossness in Jacobean drama. These two comedies of manners are quite the same in type as Brome's, but without the humor-studies. They

[1] *Cambridge Hist. Eng. Lit.* 6. 255—6.

[2] Especially Pt. 1, sc. 9. Dekker's *Works* (ed. Pearson, 2. 50—54).

[3] 4. 1, pp. 443 ff.

[4] The dialogue and jokes of the scenes at the shop of Candido in the *Honest Whore, Pt.* 1, are in a manner that Brome frequently tries, but there is no direct influence apparent.

have very complicated plots, but not so well managed
as Brome's.   They are totally without a regular organic
development of one theme : *Northward Ho*, especially,
is a string of episodes.   Brome's skill in construction
can not come from Dekker.   The influence, I think, consists in the fondness for bourgeois intrigue as a dramatic
theme, hints for the plot of the *City Wit*, and a similarity in a few characters.

In *Westward Ho* there are four intrigues of citizens'
wives with city gallants.   This I have already mentioned
as not only a favorite theme in Brome's plots, but one
which he alludes to constantly.[1]   The underplots of the
Mad Couple well Matched, *Sparagus Garden*, and *New
Exchange*, have characters that find their duplicates
in both these comedies of manners of Dekker and Webster.
The treatment of this theme and these characters, moreover, is much closer to that of *Northward Ho* and *Westward Ho* than that of the few cases found in Jonson.[2]

The last mentioned of these plays is, I think, a much
closer source for the *City Wit* than *Timon of Athens*,
which Professor Koeppel has proposed as the original.
Justiniano, the merchant, through his jealousy causes
his wife to leave him.   He then, under pretense of going
on a journey, goes about the city disguised as a writing-
master or a collier, makes a great deal of trouble for
his faithless friends and neighbors, and finally discovers
his wife's fidelity.   The merchant's character might
well have formed the basis for the character of Crasy
in the *City Wit*, and, though the motives are different,
the general scheme of a man revenging himself by tricking

---

[1] See above, p. 65.

[2] See above, p. 89.   Thomann (*Der Eifersüchtige Ehemann im
Drama der Elisabethanischen Zeit*, Halle, 1908) gives a catalogue
of examples in the miracle plays, Heywood's interludes, Lyly,
Greene, Marlowe, Jonson, Shakespeare, etc.

his friends through a series of disguises makes the resemblance quite close. The fact that several of Crasy's tricks are designed to test the fidelity of his wife adds something further to the evidence. Finally, this is the play which Fleay and Bayne agree shows most markedly the ' easy humor ' of Dekker. However, the very successful treatment of a plot of trickery in the matter of structure, as I have already suggested,[1] is due to a study of the *Alchemist*.

The most tangible indication of the borrowing of a specific character is the similarity of the wittol, Saleware, in the *Mad Couple well Matched*, to Candido, the husband in the underplot of the *Honest Whore, Part I*. Saleware refuses to be jealous of his wife, who tries her best to make him ; Candido refuses to lose his patience, though his wife lays various plots against him to force him to show some resentment.[2] Another type of character that Brome uses, which is a great favorite with Dekker, is the loud, coarse-grained, but good-natured harlot, or bawd. For instance, Bettie and Francisca, who attack each other with torrents of Billingsgate in *Covent Garden Weeded* (4. 1), and then are easily reconciled, are quite like such characters in Dekker.

I should also mention the cony-catching underplot of *Northward Ho* as a possible source for the similar theme in Brome and his contemporaries. Dol, a harlot, with the help of several men friends, cheats some foolish fellows of their money by pretending to offer herself as a wealthy ward looking for a match. This, of course, is not so close a parallel to the favorite situation of late drama, the tricking a dull country fellow who wishes to

---

[1] See above, p. 55.

[2] Faust (*op. cit.*, p. 62) works out the similarity at length. As I came to the same conclusion before reading Faust, I am convinced that this is an undoubted case of the influence of Dekker.

become a gay city blade, as is the *Alchemist*, though the difference of dates, 1605 and 1610, gives Dekker and Webster the priority. However, the possible influence of *Northward Ho* on the *Alchemist* is worth suggesting. The similarity in character of the two Dols, and the fact that two of the victims in *Northward Ho* speak foreign languages, and one in the *Alchemist* pretends that he does also, with the resulting confusion, strengthen the impression that Jonson may have borrowed this incident. Brome's introduction of Swatzenburg, the ' glorious German,' a French cavalier, and a brave Spaniard, as suitors for the advertised maidenhead of Victoria, the famous ' Novella,' in the play so called, may have been in imitation of Dekker's Hans von Belch, the Dutchman, and Captain Jenkyns, the Welshman, or of Jonson's Sir Pertinax Surly, in the guise of a Spaniard.

MINOR INFLUENCES

Beside these three important sources of influence, there are a few possibilities of borrowing from most of the other contemporaries. Some of these are extremely doubtful. Eight of the cases that have been indicated by various scholars seem worth pointing out. To these I have added eleven more.

From Massinger Brome may have received four hints, or at best, possible reminiscences. The genius who appears in the *Queen's Exchange*, Act 4, to encourage Anthynus, and help along the action by dumb show, may have been suggested by the good and bad spirits who follow two of the characters in the *Virgin Martyr*.[1] There is a general resemblance between parts of the main situations of the *New Academy* and of the *City Madam*. This consists in the plotting of a landless scoundrel with the steward of his wealthy brother to get money away

[1] Ward, *op. cit.*, 3. 129, note 4.

from the brother. Faust, I think makes too much of
this resemblance ; his closest parallel, *New Academy*
Act 1, with *City Madam* 2. 1, is not very convincing.[1]
The Bellamy episode in the *Mad Couple well Matched*
is a variation of the changeling motive of *Measure for
Measure*, but the *Parliament of Love* is nearer as a source.[2]
The similarity of the methods in which the play within
a play is introduced into the plot of the *Antipodes* and
of the *Roman Actor* will be treated at length in the consideration of the sources of the *Antipodes*.[3]

Middleton has a parallel to the pretended wealthy
Widow Tryman, who, in the *City Wit*, has several men
running after her for her money, in the courtesan in
A Trick to catch the Old One. In the *Court Begger* (2. 1,
p. 232), Citwit declines to resent an insult to his mother,
on the ground that she is dead. ' If she were living,'
he says, ' Why I would civilly ask her if she were a whore ?
If she confess'd it, then he were in the right, and I ought
not to fight against him : for my cause were naught.
If she deny'd it, then he were in an error, and his cause
were naught, and I would not fight, 'twere better he
should live to repent his error.' This passage suggests
the situation of the *Fair Quarrel*.

Fletcher and Brome seem to touch in several places.
I have already discussed their personal relations,[4] but I
think there may also be possibilities of influence. The
Begger's Bush perhaps gave a hint for the outdoor spirit
of the *Jovial Crew*.[5] With the *City Wit* 3. 1, where
Jeremy pretends to be the Widow Tryman who makes
a will on her deathbed, may be compared the *Spanish
Curate* 4. 5, where Diego does the same thing. Constance,

---

[1] Faust, *op. cit.*, pp. 63–64.
[2] Koeppel, *Shakespeare's Wirkung*, pp. 42–43 ; also *Quellen-
Studien* 2. 106 ff.
[3] See Appendix I. [4] See above, p. 20. [5] Ward, *op. cit.*, 3. 130.

in the *Northern Lass,* goes mad for love, like the jailor's daughter in the *Two Noble Kinsmen.*[1] The main situation in this same play of Fletcher's is much like that of the *Lovesick Court,* where the princess Eudina is in love with two brothers, and unable to choose between them.[2] Moreover, there is probably influence of *King and No King*[3] on the *Lovesick Court.* The sister's love for her brother (3. 2) results in much the same situation as in Fletcher—that is, it is later discovered that the pair are not brother and sister.

Ford's *'T is Pity* may possibly have suggested this theme of incest.[4] The same theme in the love of Offa for Mildred, in the *Queen's Exchange,* doubtless goes back to the same source. The strange Masque of Discord in the *Antipodes* (5. 10) indicates another influence of Ford, in the Masque of Madness in *Lover's Melancholy* (2. 3).

Shirley, in his *Lady of Pleasure* 5. 1 (1635, pr. 1637) makes the student, Frederick, when drunk, court his aunt. A similar situation occurs in the *Mad Couple well Matched* 3. 1 (1636?), where the rake Careless courts his aunt, the Lady Thrivewell, the morning after he has come in drunk, and misbehaved. The similarity of the 'academy' of deportment in the *New Academy* and that in *Lovetricks, or the School of Compliment,* I have already spoken of in connection with the possible influence of the *Staple of News* or *Cynthia's Revels.*[5]

Chapman's Cynthia, in his *Widow's Tears,* may have suggested Josina, a kind of 'Matron of Ephesus,' in the *City Wit.*[6] The green-room scene in the *Gentleman Usher*

---

[1] Ward, *op. cit.,* 3. 128.　　[2] Schelling, *Eliz. Drama* 2. 336.

[3] Faust (*op. cit.,* p. 77) mentions this as the sole source.

[4] Schelling (*Eliz. Drama* 2. 336), thinks the influence apparent enough to help determine the date of Ford's play.

[5] See above, p. p. 68, n ; 86.

[6] Koeppel, *Shakespeare's Wirkung,* p. 43 ; and *Quellen-Studien* 2. 66.

(2. 1) also bears some resemblance to that in the *Antipodes* (2. 1, p. 258).

Marmion, I think, has undoubtedly been drawn on by Brome for two scenes. The resemblance of the *English Moor* 1. 3 to the *Fine Companion* 2. 4 and 3. 5 is quite apparent. In both plays an avaricious father tries to make his young and unwilling daughter submit to a most unattractive, wealthy, old husband. The similarity of the recitals of the cures of the celebrated doctor in the *Fine Companion* (5. 2)[1] and in the *Antipodes* (1. 1, p. 234) is too close to admit much doubt of borrowing on Brome's part.

From May's *Heir* (5. 1) the *dénouement* of the *Sparagus Garden* (5. 12), in which the heroine's pregnancy is found to be due to a concealed cushion, is evidently borrowed.[2]

Finally, the Lord Sycophant, in the old play *Nobody and Somebody*, seems to have been the prototype of Horatio, one of the new characters in the *Queen and Concubine*, not taken from the source.[3]

After glancing over these many pages of borrowings and influences of all sorts, many of them doubtful, I must admit, one gets the impression that Brome's work is a mere mosaic of filchings from his predecessors, and one may be inclined to agree with Faust that ' Er ist, auch in Hinblick auf die Stoffe, vielleicht der am wenigsten selbständige dramatische Autor der Zeit.'[4] However, if a study of such material were made for any other minor dramatist of the decadent period, Brome would hardly be found the worst plagiarist in an age in which plagiarism was neither considered a crime, nor thought of as furnishing dry bones for future scholars to gnaw.

---

[1] See Appendix I.   [2] Genest, *op. cit.*, 10. 40.
[3] Koeppel, *Quellen-Studien* 2. 209.   [4] Faust, *op. cit.*, p. 37.

APPENDIX

To give a more adequate idea of the character of Brome's work, and to show more fully to what an extent he is a follower of Jonson in satire, I have added a special study of a single play, the *Antipodes*. This is undoubtedly Brome's most original and most interesting play. It is also quite characteristic in the use of sources, in the humor, and in the type of the satire. In structure, however, it is totally unlike the rest of Brome's plays, and, is in fact, almost unique in drama. The plot is as follows :

Peregrine, a young man, the son of old Joyless, has lost his wits through the reading of books of travel, so popular during the seventeenth century. He has become so demented through thinking of nothing but strange countries and customs—like those described in Sir John Mandeville's *Travels*—that he has forgotten everything else, even his duties toward his young wife, Martha. To cure his son, Joyless has brought him up to London to consult Hughball, a famous doctor, who undertakes the case. The doctor lives with Letoy, ' a Phantasticke Lord ', who, for his own amusement, keeps a well equipped private stage, and a body of followers who are trained actors. The doctor has these actors present a series of scenes from the antipodes before Peregrine, who is persuaded to believe that he is really there. Most of the second, third, and fourth acts is taken up with these scenes. In the antipodes, gentlemen in debt force sergeants to arrest them, servants rule masters, children rule their parents, poets are wealthy and Puritanical, lawyers refuse fees except from beggars, courtiers quarrel like clowns, and watermen and sedan-men have the manners of courtiers. A tradesman sues a judge to have a gentleman put into prison, because the gentleman has refused to intrigue with the trademan's wife ; an old woman who is very fond of bear-baitings is harshly reproved by a young maid, a Puritan, who reads devotional tracts. In the next scene, the maid accosts a man on the

street, but her advances are repelled   A ' man-scold ' is
ducked by a crowd of women.   A statesman is solicited by
a crowd of projectors with fantastic projects.   In the midst
of these scenes, Peregrine invades the property-room, and,
after a fight with the pasteboard monsters, etc., makes himself king of the Antipodes.   He proceeds to reform their
manners, is persuaded to take his wife, Martha, as queen, and
is finally cured of his madness.   The love-melancholy of
Martha is also cured by the long deferred consummation of
her marriage.

Another interest in the plot is the curing of Joyless's jealousy
of his young wife, Diana.   This is the chief interest of the
fifth act, though the jealousy is the cause of much humorous
dialogue all through the play.   The means of cure is crude.
Joyless is placed in a position from which he overhears Lord
Letoy make violently amorous proposals to Diana, who
repulses him by stoutly maintaining her love for Joyless.
Joyless is further convinced by the fact that Letoy is proved
to be the father of Diana, who has been brought up from
infancy by old Truelock, to whom Letoy had confided her.
After these explanations, the play ends with a masque of
Discord and Harmony.

I. SOURCES OF BROME'S *ANTIPODES*

The scientific fact of the existence of the antipodes and of
people inhabiting there seems to have been known to Aristotle,
and to many other writers of classical antiquity.[1]   Cicero,
Pliny,[2] and Ptolemy supported the theory ; Lucretius and
Plutarch opposed it.   The conception persisted as a heretical
belief throughout the Middle Ages, so that the Fathers felt
it necessary to suppress it whenever it appeared.   A good
summary of the controversies of the church on the subject
is given by Andrew D. White in his *Warfare of Science and*

[1] The Pauly-Wissowa *Real-Encyclopädie des Class. Altertums,*
under *Antipodes,* gives a long array of references.
[2] *Natural History,* Bk. 2, ch. 65.

Theology (p. 103). A very interesting old book that Brome
might have seen, José Acosta's *Natural and Moral History
of the Indies*, translated by Edward Grimeston, London,
1604,[1] has two curious chapters[2] on the existence of the antipodes. He says : ' Seeing it is manifest that there is firme
land upon the South part or Pole Antartike, wee must now
see if it be inhabited ; the which hath been a matter very
disputable in former times. Lactantius Firmian and S. Augustine mocke at such as hold there be any Antipodes, which
is as much as to say, as men marching with their feete opposite
to ours. But although these two authors agree in these
jeasts, yet doe they differ much in their reasons and opinions,
as they were of very divers spirits and judgements. Lactantius
followes the vulgar, seeming ridiculous unto to him that the
heaven should be compassed in the midst thereof, like unto
a ball, whereof he writes in these tearmes : " What reason
is there for some to affirm that there are Antipodes, whose
steppes are opposite to ours ? Is it possible that any should
bee so grosse and simple as to believe there were a people or
nation marching with their feete upwards, and their heades
downwards, and that things which are placed heere of one sort,
are in that other part hanging topsie turvie ; that trees and
corne growe downwards, and that raine, snow, and haile,
fall from the earth upward." Then, after some other discourse,
the same Lactantius useth these words : " The imagination
and conceit which some have had, supposing the heavens to be
round, hath bene the cause to invent these Antipodes hanging
in the aire. So as I know not what to say of such Philosophers,
whoe having once erred, continue still obstinately in their
opinions defending one another." But whatsoever he saieth,
wee that live now at Peru, and inhabite that part of the world
which is opposite to Asia and their Antipodes (as the Cosmo-
graphers do teach us) find not our selves to bee hanging in
the aire, our heades downwards and our feete on high. Truly
it is strange to consider that the spirit and understanding
of man cannot attaine unto the trueth, without the use of

[1] Reprinted by the Hakluyt Society, 1880.
[2] Bk. 1, Chaps. 7 and 8.

imagination.' Acosta then goes on to refute St. Augustine's attack, which was based upon the authority of Scripture. This view the Church considered final until Magellan in 1519 disproved it by circumnavigating the earth, and seeing the inhabitants of the antipodes.

None of these ancient ideas on the subject, however, as far as I have been able to discover, include the suggestion of topsyturvydom upon which Brome has based his comedy. Moreover, I have not been able to find that any such idea was ever associated with the antipodes before the date of this play. The following definition, quoted from a dictionary of the seventeenth century, shows that the belief accepted then was in the same form as we hold it to-day, without any fantastic notion accompanying it [1] : ' Antipodes, (Gr.) people dwelling on the other side of the earth with their feet directly against ours, so as a right line drawn from one to the other passeth from North to South, through the centre of the world. They are different 180 degrees, which is half the compass of the earth. They differ in all things, as seasons of the year, length of days, rising and setting of the sun, with the like. Heyl. [Dr. Heylyn].' In eighteen [2] other uses of the word that I have chanced upon in reading in the period, there is no hint that the idea suggested anything more than this definition implies. One further indication of the same view is the fact that Sir Thomas Browne, who alludes to the antipodes, has no hint of the reversal of the ordinary relations of life, or of physical phenomena. If the conception back of Brome's play were known to Browne, it would represent a vulgar error that it would have delighted him to refute. The only suggestion of such an association with the word occurs in a poem of 1657, called the *Parliament*.[3] The passage reads :

[1] *Glossographia*, by T. B., 1656.

[2] These references occur in plays, poems, letters, and pamphlets from 1590 to 1650.

[3] Printed from a MS. in Huth's *Inedited Poetical Misscellanies*, 1584—1700.

And yet a drayman may advance
Yet to be styled your honour ;
A braver fortune doth enhance,
And highness take upon her.
Here's the Antipodes or nowhere ;
The Upper House becomes the Lower.

This quotation is hardly of much importance, particularly as it occurs long after the date of the play, but I give it because it is the nearest hint of the idea under discussion.

As a result of this evidence, I think we must allow Brome's fantastic conception of the antipodes to be his own. A few suggestions, however, of topsyturvydom used with comic effect may be brought forward as possible germs of the idea that he developed with much cleverness and originality. Ward [1] remarks that 'perhaps he had been looking into Bacon's *New Atlantic* (published 1627), or he may have derived a general hint from Jonson's masque of the *World in the Moon* (1620).' Faust's comment on this is [2]: ' Dass Brome die Idee zur Schilderung solch einer verkehrten Welt durch Jonsons Maske *News from the New World discovered in the Moon* empfangen habe, was Ward für wahrscheinlich hält, kann nicht ohne weiteres geleugnet werden; nur ist zu bedenken, dass beiden Dichtungen kaum ein individueller Zug gemein ist. Auch Bacon's *New Atlantis* könnte höchstens eine Anregung genereller Art gegeben haben.' In this scientist's paradise of Bacon's I can find nothing that could suggest itself as a parallel to Brome's play   The idea of a voyage to a strange land, whose customs differ in some ways from the English, is all they have in common. The nearest hint to be found in Jonson's masque is in coaches that go only with wind, coachmen ' with cheeks like a trumpeter ' to blow them along, walks in the clouds, epicoenes who lay eggs, and children who are part fowl.

Jonson's masque has been shown to have been based partly on Lucian's *Vera Historia*,[3] which may possibly have

[1] *Op. cit.*, 3. 130.   [2] *Op. cit.*, p. 57.
[3] J. Q. Adams, *Mod. Lang. Notes* 19. 1—3.

given some suggestion to Brome as well. Most of the wonders in the *Vera Historia* are wildly fantastic ideas like those quoted from Jonson, but occasionally they occur as usages or views exactly antipodal to our own. Such a notion appears in the description of the inhabitants of the moon [1] : ' Beauty with them consists in a bald head and hairless body ; a good crop of hair is an abomination. On the comets, as I was told by some of their inhabitants who were there on a visit, this is reversed.' There are other passages like this, but none which show definitely that Brome actually took any suggestion from Lucian.

A much more definite suggestion, and in fact, an undoubted source for at least part of the conception of the antipodes, is to be found in the *Late Lancashire Witches*. Here there is a scene in which, through witchcraft, the usual relations of father and son are completely reversed. The son keeps his father on an allowance and reproves him severely for his extravagance, and the father, in great awe of his son, meekly begs forgiveness. This scene is closely imitated in *Antipodes* 2. 9, where three old men carrying satchels like school-boys, enter singing, ' Domine, domine, duster ! Three knaves in a cluster ! ' The son of one of them rebukes them severely for playing truant, and they all reluctantly go off to school. The scene in the *Lancashire Witches* from which this is copied is one that I have attributed to Heywood.[2] This is one source, at least, with which we have positive proof that Brome was thoroughly acquainted. It may be that the whole conception of the play was developed from this scene, the success of which with the public Brome had, of course, opportunities of testing.

One more possible source for the underlying idea of the *Antipodes* is the *Travels of Sir John Mandeville*. This popular old collection of cock-and-bull stories about far countries is mentioned by name in the play, and frequently quoted and alluded to. It is not at all improbable that the extraordinary customs of the strange peoples described

[1] H. W. and F. G. Fowler's *Translation of Lucian* 2. 145.
[2] See above, p. 51.

in that delightful old book may have suggested to Brome the possibilities of fun and satire in an inverted world. The existence of the antipodes is implied in chapter 20 [1] : ' And wit well, that, after that I may perceive and comprehend, the lands of Prester John, Emperor of Ind, be under us. For in going from Scotland or from England toward Jerusalem men go upward always. For our land is in the low part of the earth toward the west, and the land of Prester John is in the low part of the earth toward the east. And [they] have there the day when we have the night ; also, high to the contrary, they have the night when we have the day. For the earth and the sea be of round form and shape, as I have said before ; and that that men go upward to one coast, men go downward to another coast.'

Having arrived at this idea of the antipodes, Brome may have associated with it some of the marvels of other lands in Mandeville. For instance, in chapter 31 an isle is mentioned where women sorrow when children are born, and rejoice when they die.[2] The godly souls of the Isle of Bragenan in chapter 32 [3] must also have appealed to the satirist. ' In that isle is no thief, ne murderer, ne common woman, ne poor beggar, ne never was man slain in that country. And they be so chaste, and lead so good life, as that they were religious men. And because they be so true and so rightful, and so full of all good conditions, they were never grieved with tempests, ne with thunder, ne with light, ne with hail, ne with pestilence, ne with war, ne with hunger, ne with none other tribulation, as we be many times, amongst us, for our sins.'

Whether or not Brome drew from Pseudo-Mandeville the fundamental conception of his play, he used the *Travels* as his only source for the deranged Peregrine's conversations on the wonders of distant parts. I find, in all, seven passages taken directly from this source. The first parallel is almost an attempted quotation, but all the others merely allusions to the idea in Mandeville :

[1] Ed. 1905, p. 122.   [2] *Op. cit.*, p. 189.   [3] *Op. cit.*, p. 192.

He talks much of the Kingdome of *Cathaya*,
Of one great *Caan*, and goodman *Prester Iohn*,
(What e're they be) and sayes that *Caan's* a Clowne
Unto the *Iohn* he speaks of.　And that *Iohn*
Dwels up almost at Paradice : But sure his mind
Is in a wildernesse : For there he sayes
Are Geese that have two heads a peece, and Hens
That beare more wooll upon their backs than sheep.
. . . .
And men with heads like hounds.
　　　　　　　　　　　　　(*Antipodes* 1. 3, p. 240)

With this passage compare the following three from Mandeville : ' Under the firmament is not so great a lord, ne so
mighty, ne so rich as is the great Chan ; not Prester John,
that is Emperor of the high Ind, ne the Soldan of Babylon,
ne the Emperor of Persia.　All these be not in comparison
to the great Chan, neither of might, ne of noblesse, ne of
royalty, ne of riches ; for in all these he passeth all earthly
princes.'
　　　　　　　　　　　　　(Chap. 25, p. 161)

'In that country be white hens without feathers, but they
bear white wool as sheep do here.'
　　　　　　　　　　　　　(Chap. 22, p. 136)

'And all the men and women of the isle have hound's
heads, and they be clept Cynocephales.'
　　　　　　　　　　　　　Chap. 21, p. 130)

Peregrine.
And seen the trees of the Sunne and Moone, that speake.
And told King Alexander of his death,
Ha you bin there Sir, ha' you seene those trees ?
Doctor.　And talked with hem, and tasted of their fruit.
Peregrine.　Read here againe then : it is written here,
That you may live foure or five hundred yeere.
　　　　　　　　　　　　　'(*Antipodes*, 1. 6, p. 248—9)

Compare : 'But it was told us of them of the country, that
within those deserts were the trees of the Sun and of the
Moon, that spoke to King Alexander, and warned him of
his death.　And men say that the folk who keep those
trees, and eat of the fruit and of the balm that groweth

there, live well four hundred year or five hundred year by
virtue of the fruit and of the balm.'

(Chap. 32. p. 196)

. . . Are they not such
As *Mandevile* writes of without heads or necks,
Having their eyes plac'd on their shoulders, and
Their mouths amidst their breasts ?

(*Antipodes*, 1. 6, p. 250)

Compare : ' And in another isle toward the south dwell folk
of foul stature and of cursed kind that have no heads.
And their eyen be in their shoulders.' [1]

(Chap. 22, p, 133)

Mandivell writes
Of peopel near the *Antipodes*, called *Gadlibriens* :
Where on the wedding-night the husband hires
Another man to couple with his bride,
To clear the dangerous passage of a Maidenhead.

. . . .

She may be of that Serpentine generation
That stings oft times to death (as Mandevile writes).

(4. 10. p. 315)

The source of this is the following passage in Mandeville.
(Chap. 31, p. 188):

'Another isle is there, full fair and good and great, and
full of people, where the custom is such, that the first night
that they be married, they make another man to lie by their
wives for to have their maidenhead : and therefore they
take great hire and great thank. And there be certain
men in every town that serve of none other thing ; and
they clepe them Cadeberiz, that is to say the fools of wanhope.
For they of the country hold it so great a thing and so perilous
for to have the maidenhead of a woman, that them seemeth
that they that have first the maidenhead putteth him in
adventure of his life. And if the husband find his wife
maiden that other next night after that she should have been
lain by of the man that is assigned therefore, peradventure

---

[1] Cf. also *Othello* 1. 3. 144.

Anthropaphagi and men whose heads
Do grow beneath their shoulders.

for drunkeness or for some other cause, the husband shall plain upon him that he hath not done his devoir, in such cruel wise as though the officers would have slain him. But after the first night that they be lain by, they keep them so straitly that they be not so hardy to speak with no man. And I asked them the cause why that they held such a custom : and they said me, that of old time men had been dead for deflowering of maidens, that had serpents in their bodies that stung men upon their yards, that they died anon : and therefore they held that custom, to make other men ordained therefore to lie by their wives, for dread of death, and to assay the passage of another [rather] than for to put them in that adventure.'

Before leaving this matter of the relation of Mandeville to Brome, I must mention the occurrence in Schelling's list [1] of a play called *Sir John Maundeville*, which is alluded to by Henslowe [2] in 1592. As this is all that is known of the play, it is idle to conjecture whether there was any relation between it and the *Antipodes*.

Another important element on which the play depends, more a matter of structure than of subject-matter, is the dramatic device of presenting a play within a play. There are many parallel cases of this in Elizabethan drama, from the *Spanish Tragedy* down.[3] The device must have been very familiar to Brome, for I have run across seven or eight cases of its use in the plays I am familiar with. We may add to these the large number of plays that contain elaborate masques.

In Middleton's *Mayor of Queenborough* (c. 1596) 5. 1, a company of strolling players come in and give a scene of horse-play as an interlude for the amusement of the mayor, but the scene is purely outside the main action of the piece. A more elaborate one is presented by a body of masquers in Chapman's *Gentleman Usher* (c. 1601) 2. 1, but here again we have the disconnected interest of an interlude in the

---

[1] *Op. cit.*, 2. 587. [2] *Henslowe's Diary*, ed. Greg, p. 13.
[3] Dr. H. Schwab has briefly treated a few such plays in *Das Schauspiel im Schauspiel* (1896).

plot. The play in the fifth act of *Midsummer Night's Dream* bears the same relation to the main plot. The only example in Jonson of this sort of thing is the long masque of 'five motions' that concludes the *Tale of a Tub* (? 1601). But this masque is far from being connected with the main plot, which it merely summarizes, and is added after the conclusion of the real action of the play. In Shirley's *Traitor* (1631) 3. 2, there is a short play, which, though it does not form an integral part of the plot, fits into it very well, and contributes to the atmosphere. Occurring in the middle of the play, it partly reviews the antecedent action, like the Mouse-Trap in *Hamlet*, and partly foreshadows the revenge to come.

All of these pieces, however, have nothing in common with the *Antipodes* except the idea of a play within a play. But there are a half dozen of the older plays which use this device as an important integral part of the whole plot. The *Spanish Tragedy* (1586) 4. 3, and *Hamlet* (1602) 3. 2, are of course the most obvious examples, which must have influenced considerably all later attempts at this sort of thing in drama. Middleton and Rowley's *Spanish Gipsy* (1623) 4. 3 uses the play within a play in much the same manner, so that through the influence of the scene on the spectator for whom it is devised the resolution of one of the interests of the plot is brought about. The two first-mentioned plays of this type were, of course, well known to Brome, and Faust's proof that the *Spanish Gipsy* is the main source of the *Jovial Crew* [1] shows that this other case of an included play was known as well.

Though these examples may be considered as a sort of precedent for Brome, there are three more uses of the same dramatic idea that are close enough parallels to be looked upon almost as direct suggestions, if not actual sources. In structure, Randolph's *Muses' Looking-Glass* (1634) is so much like the *Antipodes* that we may say that together they form a special type, of which, as far as I know, there are no other examples in the period. Both consist for the

[1] Faust, *op. cit.*, p. 85.

greater part of a series of disconnected scenes, which form a loose kind of play within a rather slight framework. The *Taming of the Shrew* is hardly of the same type, because the framework is connected only mechanically with the included play, which is a complete drama in itself. The resemblance of the *Antipodes* and the *Muses' Looking-Glass* ceases at the similarity of structure. Randolph's comedy is more serious in its purpose, didactic in its point of view, and less interesting in theme and treatment than the clever farce of Brome, with fun for its only aim.

Another play of the same general type as we have been discussing, but quite different in structure from the two last mentioned, is the one in Massinger's *Roman Actor* (1626) 2. 1. Here the Emperor Domitianus attempts the cure of the rich miser Philargus by having the players give a short play in which a miser is shown his own folly, and cured. Old Philargus takes the representation very seriously, and loses himself in interest, just as Peregrine and Martha do in the *Antipodes*, but, unlike them, he is not cured by the emperor's device. In the same play further on (3. 2), the Empress Domitia, in witnessing another little piece, forgets that Paris, the Roman actor, is acting, and betrays her love and anxiety for him, just as Diana and the more naïve Martha openly express their admiration for the characters on the antipodean stage. Finally, in 4. 2, the masque in the *Roman Actor* becomes a reality, a tragic one however, just as the comic antipodean play merges, toward the end, into the main plot or framework of Brome's piece. The comparison of the two plays adds another possible reminiscence of Massinger in Brome to that of the appearance of the genius in both the *Virgin Martyr* (1620) and the *Queens' Exchange* (1631), noted by Ward.[1]

Finally, there is one more close parallel of a play, or rather a masque, within a play which is intended to operate as a cure on one of the characters in the main plot. In Ford's *Lover's Melancholy* (1628) 3. 3, the physician Corax presents a strange masque, representing six different kinds of melancholy, before the Prince Palador, in order to make him realize how foolish

[1] *Op. cit.*, 3. 129, note 4.

his own affliction of love-melancholy seems to others, so that a cure may be brought about. The method of Corax here, and in his treatment of Meleander, the old, partly demented father of Eroclea, later in the play, is the sort of mind-cure, the method of the 'Emmanuel Movement,' that is employed by the physician in the *Antipodes*.

We need not, however, from this similarity, assume any influence of Ford's play on Brome. The masque in *Lover's Melancholy* is really a dramatization of passages from Burton's *Anatomy of Melancholy* (1621), which is, in fact, the source of the whole play. I think it very probable that the doctors in both plays are practitioners of the school of Burton. There are several passages in the *Anatomy of Melancholy* that might well have been the starting-point for Massinger, Ford, and Brome independently. Cures of the sort we are discussing would come under the head of 'artificial inventions' for rectifying the mind afflicted with some kind of 'melancholy.' ' Sometimes again by some feigned lie, strange news, witty device, artificial invention, it is not amiss to deceive them,'[1] says Burton, who afterwards cites several strange cures of ' passions and perturbations of the mind.' None of them, however, directly suggest the method of the *Antipodes*. In another place, Martha's affliction and the means of her cure, are hinted at[2] : ' The several cures of this infirmity [women's melancholy], concerning diet, which must be very sparing, phlebotomy, physick, internal, external remedies, are at large in great variety in *Rodericus à Castro, Sennertus*, and *Mercatus*, which whosoe will, as occasion serves, may make use of. But the best and surest remedy of all is to see them well placed, and married to good husbands in due time ; *hinc illæ lachrymæ*, that is the primary cause, and this the ready cure, to give them content to their desires.' The fact that Brome was familiar with this passage from Burton is proved by a comparison of six lines of the play (1. 2, p. 239) with another passage in the same ' subsection ' of Burton on the preceding page :

[1] Part 2, *Sect.* 2, *Mem.* 6, *Subs.* 2.
[2] *Part* 1, *Sect.* 3, *Mem.* 2, *Subs.* 4.

Indeed she's full of passion, which she utters
By the effects as diversly, as severall
Objects reflect upon her wandering fancy,
Sometimes in extream weepings, and anon
In vehement laughter ; now in sullen silence,
And presently in loudest exclamations.

This is a paraphrase of the following *Symptoms of Maids', Nuns', and Widows' Melancholy* :

' And from hence proceed . . . a foolish kind of bashfulness to some, perverse conceits and opinions, dejection of mind, much discontent, preposterous judgment. They are apt to loathe, dislike, disdain, to be weary of every object, etc., each thing almost is tedious to them, they pine away, void of counsel, apt to weep, and tremble, timorous, fearful, sad, and out of all hope of better fortunes. . . . And thus they are affected so long as this vapour lasteth ; but by and by as pleasant and merry as ever they were in their lives, they sing, discourse and laugh in any good company, upon all occasions, and so by fits it takes them now and then.'

Dr. Faust has mentioned another source for, or parallel to the method of curing Peregrine. He says : [1] ' Die Kurmethode, welche der Arzt bei Peregrin anwendet, war nichts Neues im Drama ; es ist doch dieselbe, deren sich der Doktor in the *Two Noble Kinsmen* bedient, um des Kerkermeisters Tochter wieder zur Vernunft zu bringen : scheinbares Eingehen auf die Wahnideen des Patienten.' There are two scenes of the *Two Noble Kinsmen*, 4. 3 and 5. 2, that I think are interesting parallels for the cure of Martha, but hardly close enough to indicate any direct influence. The doctor here again puts into practice Burton's principles for the cure of love-melancholy.[2]

[1] *Op. cit.*, p. 59.

[2] The fact that the doctor in this underplot follows Burton's ideas closely may have some bearing on the question of the double authorship of the *Two Noble Kinsmen*. Hickson and Fleay divide the underplot between Shakespeare and Fletcher, giving 4. 3 to Shakespeare, and 5. 2 to Fletcher. Spalding gives the whole underplot to Fletcher (Rolfe's ed., p. 39 and notes, pp. 190 and 195). Now Shakespeare's part was written. of course, before the *Anatomy of*

The distraction of the jailer's daughter, which is as extreme as that of Ophelia, is caused by an unrequited passion for Palamon, of whom she talks continually. She is cured by soft lights, pleasant odors, sleep, etc., and by having her wooer impersonate Palamon. After the consummation of her marriage the madness disappears. It is only in this last-mentioned detail that the plot agrees with that of the *Antipodes*.[1]

Of minor influences discernible in the play we have the two marked Jonsonian humor-characters, Letoy and Joyless. Letoy, the ' fantastick lord ' who is very conscious of his eccentricities, has no prototype in Jonson, but Brome has compounded his character after the recipe of the master. For Joyless, the groundlessly jealous husband, there are, of course, many precedents outside of Jonson, but in Kitely in *Every Man in his Humor* we have the same characteristic exaggerated for comic effect, that we see in Brome's absurd creation. Kitely, in the first scene of the second act in Jonson's play, regrets his own jealously as a disease from which he suffers, much as Joyless does in the last act of the *Antipodes*. Jonson's influence is further discernible in the introduction of projectors in 4. 9 (pp. 308 ff).

Finally, there are three passages in the play that seem to be conscious verbal imitations. The scene in which Blaze tells Joyless of the doctor's famous cures (1. 1, pp. 234 ff.) is very like one in Marmion's *Fine Companion* (1633) 5. 2, where Aurelio disguised as a doctor tells how, without the aid of drugs, he cured the madness of an astrologer, a soldier, a Puritan chandler, a musician, a huntsman, and a poet. Letoy's advice to his actors in 2. 2 is undoubtedly reminiscent of

---

Melancholy (Schelling says 1612), but Fletcher, writing in 1625 (Fleay), four years after its appearance, may have been influenced by it. This might be a further argument for Spalding's view.

[1] The madness of Peregrine and Martha is but one of several examples of different kinds of insanity in Brome's plays. It occurs in some form in *Northern Lass*, *Queen's Exchange*, *Court Begger*, and *Queen and Concubine*.

Hamlet's speech to his players.[1] Both are directed against bombastic acting and interpolations into the text.

The passage from Brome is worth quoting in full :

> *Let.* Let me not see you act now,
> In your Scholasticke way, you brought to towne wi'yee,
> With see saw sacke a downe, like a Sawyer ;
> Nor in a Comicke Scene, play *Hercules furens,*
> Tearing your throat to split the Audients eares.
> And you Sir, you had got a tricke of late,
> Of holding out your bum in a set speech ;
> Your fingers fibulating on your breast,
> As if your Buttons, or your Band-strings were
> Helpes to your memory. Let me see you in't
> No more I charge you. No, nor you sir, in
> That over-action of the legges I told you of,
> Your singles, and your doubles, Looke you—thus—
> Like one o'th' dancing Masters o'the Beare-garden ;
> And when you have spoke, at end of every speech,
> Not minding the reply, you turne you round
> As Tumblers doe ; when betwixt every feat
> They gather wind, by firking up their breeches.
> Ile none of these absurdities in my house,
> But words and action married so together,
> That shall strike harmony in the eares and eyes
> Of the severest, if judicious Criticks.
>   *Qua.* My Lord we are corrected.
>   *Let.*   Goe, be ready :
> But you Sir are incorrigible, and
> Take licence to your selfe, to adde unto
> Your parts, your owne free fancy ; and sometimes
> To alter, or diminish what the writer
> With care and skill compos'd : and when you are
> To speake to your coactors in the Scene,
> You hold interloquutions with the Audients.
>   *Bip.* That is a way my Lord has bin allow'd
> On elder stages to move mirth and laughter.
>   *Let.* Yes in the dayes of *Tarlton* and *Kempe,*
> Before the stage was purg'd from barbarisme,
> And brought to the perfection it now shines with.

---

[1] *Hamlet* 3. 2. Compare also Chapman's *Gentleman Usher* (1601 or 1602) 2. 1. 170.

> Then fooles and jesters spent their wits, because
> The Poets were wise enough to save their owne
> For profitabler uses. Let that passe.

The last example of borrowing to be pointed out is that in the passage in which Letoy tells of his ancestry (1. 5, p. 244). Here there is a close verbal reminiscence of Lafoole's in the *Silent Woman* 1. 4.[1]

By way of summary of the investigation of Brome's sources in the *Antipodes*, I think we may conclude that he deserves the credit of originating the idea at the basis of his comedy, possibly acting on the slight suggestions to be found for it in Jonson's masque, Lucian's *Vera Historia*, or in Mandeville. This last source he made free use of, at any rate, though possibly not as the germ of his idea. For the play within a play as a means of curing mental derangement, the *Roman Actor* is the most probable precedent, though the idea is to be found in the *Anatomy of Melancholy*, and two more dramas beside the one mentioned. Of minor imitations of passages the surest cases are those from Burton, Shakespeare, Jonson, and Marmion.

II. THE SATIRE OF THE *ANTIPODES*

Brome, following the principle of Jonson, is wholly impersonal in his satire. Jonson declared that he himself never departed from this principle, but it would be difficult to deny that in the *Poetaster* he actually did satirize individuals. Brome, however, although he of course has frequent allusions to contemporaries like Coryat and Prynne, has never in any of his extant plays characterized any but types or classes of men. The *Antipodes* has more satire in it than any other of his works, but the fun here is always of the most good-natured sort.

Some of the minor points that are touched on satirically in the *Antipodes* are the ranting delivery and extemporal

[1] Quoted above, p. 96.

interpolation of contemporary actors,[1] mentioned above, and the loose conduct of young gentlemen with the wives of citizen-tradesmen.[2] This last mentioned theme occurs as an episode or an underplot in the *New Academy, Sparagus Garden, City Wit*, and *Mad Couple*, and is touched on in the *Court Begger* (1. 1, p. 194), where there is a ' project ' mentioned to prevent cavaliers and courtiers from mixing with tradesmen's wives. Then there are humorous hits at poets for their poverty and reckless living[3]—the sort of fun at the author's expense that most of the playwrights seemed willing to make.

The stilted language[4] of the courtier, and his affected courtesy, were very obvious marks for the satirist. Brome makes fun of the same thing in the *Sparagus Garden* (4. 9, 10) and the *New Academy* (4. 2). This does not mean that the bourgeois poet is ridiculing the elegance and greater correctness of usage of a sphere above his own, but rather that he is deriding a relic of Euphuism that seems to have persisted in the language of courtesy. Brome is here following Jonson, who satirized the same tendency in *Cynthia's Revels*. Other examples are to be found in Newcastle's *Captain Underwit* (2. 2), Shirley's *Lady of Pleasure* (5. 1), and *Lovetricks*.

The legal profession was in the seventeenth century, as it has been before and since, a favorite target for satirical shafts. The character-books did not spare them, and the drama was particularly violent in its attacks. A study of lawyers as dramatic characters has been made by Dr. H. Bormann in his thesis, *Der Jurist im Drama der Elisabethanischen Zeit* (Halle, 1906). Brome makes sly hits at the profession in short passages in *Covent Garden Weeded* (2. 1) and the *Sparagus Garden* (5. 1).[5] Here, again, Jonson may be considered as the

[1] 2. 2, p. 250.

[2] 2. 7; 3. 8. The same old joke occurs in Massinger's *Fatal Dowry* 4. 3, ' The Courtier's Song of the Citizens ' (Marmion's *Fine Companion* 2. 2), and Nabbes' *Tottenham Court*. Middleton and Dekker's *Roaring Girl* 2. 1 gives a very realistic picture of the manners of a wife in her husband's shop.

[3] 1. 6, p. 254, and 3. 2.   [4] 3. 5; 4. 7.

[5] The justice is introduced as a comic figure in the *Damoiselle, Northern Lass*, and *Jovial Crew*.

readiest example for Brome, if he needed any predecessor at all to show him the possibilities of the theme. Jonson makes fun of lawyers in his *Epigrams*, and, in some form, either by introducing them as characters, or by directing witty remarks against them, in eight plays.[1]

Brome's satire on the lawyers in the *Antipodes*[2] is rather commonplace. It is brought in purely for the humor of the inversions, with apparently little animosity to the profession. The harshest comment is

> The lawes the river, ist ? Yes tis a river,
> Through which great men, and cunning wade or swimme,
> But meane and ignorant must drowne in't.[3]

The Puritans, natural enemies of the playwrights, were undoubtedly ridiculed by them more than any other class of people. It is useless to discuss the question here, for Dr. E. N. S. Thompson, in his *Controversy between the Puritans and the Stage*,[4] has given it detailed consideration. In satirizing them, Brome is following the lead of practically all the comic dramatists. He has really added nothing new in the way of abuse. This is also true of the rest of the Caroline dramatists. In fact, after Middleton and Jonson had finished their work, there was really nothing that could be added. Brome repeats some of the points for which Jonson had satirized the Puritans in the *Alchemist, Bartholomew Fair*, and the *Sad Shepherd*. Jonson made fun of their dress ; strange long names ; fondness for large and solemn language ; sophistry ; the narrowness, which, because of its own virtue, objected to cakes and ale ; and he even made against them the more serious accusations of hypocrisy and dishonesty.[5] Brome, in *Covent Garden Weeded*, has drawn a typical stage-Puritan, Gabriel. He whines through his nose, hates the

---

[1] Bormann omits mention of the satire in the *Silent Woman* and the *Poetaster*. See also *Magnetic Lady* (second intermean).

[2] 1. 6, p. 254; 3. 2, 3, 4, 5.   [3] 4. 4, p. 301.

[4] *Yale Studies*, No. 20.

[5] See C. S. Alden's edition of *Bartholomew Fair*, Introduction, pp. xx ff.

sight of a cross on a church because it is an ' idolatrous painted image,' and is as hypocritical as Tribulation Wholesome. In the *Mad Couple well Matched* (1. 1), a character is described as a ' Methodicall, Grave and Orthographicall speaking friend, Mr. Saveall that calls People Pe-o-ple.'

The Puritan in the *Antipodes*[1] further follows Jonson's precedent. The sober young maid objects to her grandmother's interest in bear-baitings, and calls them ' prophane and Diabolicall courses.' ' Let me entreat you,' she continues, ' Forbeare such beastly pastimes, th' are Sathanicall.' This young Puritan also reads devotional books. But in spite of this godly exterior, the ' blood rebells against the spirit,' and in the very next scene she accosts a man on the street. Here we have the hypocrisy of which Jonson accuses the Puritans. Besides the ridicule in these scenes, there are scattered allusions with the same purport. The poet[2] turns the ' godly life and death of Mistris *Katherine Stubs* ' into metre for an alderman's son to woo an ancient lady with. In the antipodes ' all their Poets are Puritanes '[3] ; Joyless' fear that his wife may fall in love with an actor at the play[4] is exactly the Puritan attitude.[5]

In all the things satirized by Brome that we have mentioned thus far, he is ridiculing rather obvious follies, without any evident endeavor to reform them. In his satire on the projectors,[6] however, he is dealing with a serious abuse of his time, the satiric treatment of which may have contributed to its reform. The monopoly system, to which these projectors belonged, was the granting to certain individuals the right of manufacture of and exclusive trade in certain things, often articles of the most common utility. For instance, among the monopolies granted in the reign of James I, are those on flasks and cartridge-boxes, for the transportation of horns for twenty-one years, to buy and bring in anise seed for twenty-one years, to buy and transport ashes and old shoes for seven years, to make spangles, to print the *Psalms of David*,

---

[1] 4. 1, 2, 3.   [2] 3. 2, p. 277.   [3] 1. 6, p. 254.   [4] 2. 9, p. 272.
[5] E. N. S. Thompson, *op. cit.*, p. 229.   [6] 4. 9.

to sow wood in a certain number of shires.[1]   Of course the granting of royal patents for such articles brought large revenues to the Crown, but also great abuses to the public. As the result of protests from Parliament, the monopolies were twice abolished in the reigns of Elizabeth and James I., but the system persisted, and continued to be a matter of contention, for many years afterward.[2]

Dr. W. S. Johnson, in the introduction to his edition of the *Devil is an Ass*,[3] gives a rather full and very excellent discussion of the system, which is the chief object of satire in that play.   Other satiric treatments of the theme mentioned by him are :

> Randolph's *Muses' Looking-Glass* (Dodsley 9. 180).
> Marmion's *Holland's Leager* 1. 5.
> Brome's *Court Begger*.
> Wilson's *The Projectors*.
> Taylor's *The Complaint of M. Tenterhook, the Projector,*
>   and *Sir Thomas Dodger, the Patentee.*

Dr. Johnson says that that in the *Devil is an Ass* (1616) is probably the earliest dramatic representation of the projector ; and, moreover, that the later appearances in the plays just mentioned lack ' the timeliness of Jonson's satire, and the conception must have been largely derived from literary sources.'   Now it is undoubtedly true that Brome and the rest are following Jonson in this point of satire,[4] which appears again in a slighter form in the character of Sir Politick Wouldbe in *Volpone*, and also in the *Masque of Augurs*. However, in saying that monopolies were no longer a political

[1] E. Lodge, *Illustrations of British Hist.* (1838) 3. 6. Price (see note 2) gives lists of monopolies in Appendices B to G.

[2] Dr. W. H. Price's *English Patents of Monopoly*, Boston, 1906, is a complete setting forth of the whole subject from the historical and economic point of view.   It says nothing of the satire of the dramatists.

[3] P. viii.

[4] Cf. the list of projects in the *Devil is an Ass* : draining the drowned lands, turning dog-skins into Spanish leather, bottling of ale, making wine of raisins or blackberries.

issue, Dr. Johnson is undoubtedly mistaken. Gardner states[1] that the monopoly act of 1621 had merely done away with private projectors, corporations being distinctly excluded from the incidence of the act. The king, therefore, had it in his power to create monopolies, by placing the sole right of manufacture in the hands of corporations. From 1631 to 1635 the monopoly on soap actually became an issue in affairs of state.[2] It was doubtless the wrangle caused by this that made the satire of Brome and other late dramatists timely. For the purpose of dramatic presentation, or perhaps as the result of the establishing of a type of humor-character by Jonson, the individual projector continued to be brought on the stage, though he now represented a corporation.

Shirley introduces into his masque, the *Triumph of Peace* (1633/4), a number of projectors, the same broad caricatures that Brome employs. Dyce's note from a contemporary source, Whitlock's *Memorials*, shows that monopolies were still a great abuse, which statesmen were trying to reform. After describing the antimasque in some detail, Whitlock says[3] : ' Several other Projectors were in like manner perso nated in this Antimasque ; and it pleased the spectators the more, because by it an information was covertly given to the King of the unfitness and ridiculousness of these projects against the law ; and the Attorney Noy, who had most knowledge of them, had a great hand in this Antimasque of the Projectors. Strafford's *Letters* (1. 167), cited by P. Reyher,[4] show further the persistance of the monopolies at this same time.

For proof that the *Antipodes* is not even three or four years late in its satire, we have Gardner's further statement that there were more corporations erected in 1636.[5] This caused great discontent, which brought about the finishing stroke to monopolies, dealt by the Long Parliament in Nov., 1640.[6]

---

[1] *Personal Government of Chas. I.* 2. 165–171.
[2] See also Price, *op. cit.*, pp. 118–128.   [3] *Memorials*, p. 20, b.
[4] *Les Masques Anglais*, p. 251. The whole subject of projectors is excellently treated here.
[5] Gardener, *op. cit.* 2. 313.   [6] Price, *op. cit.*, p. 45.

Brome has made use of this theme in a few other plays. There are two bare allusions in the *Damoiselle* (1. 1, p. 380) and the *Queen's Exchange* (3. 1, p. 502). But his most important treatment of the subject is the *Court Begger*, which seems to have been written during the very year that preceded the final abolition of the abuse. This play centres chiefly in a projector, and treats the theme with much wit and cleverness.

Other treatments of the projector by contemporaries, not yet mentioned, are Massinger's *Emperor of the East* ; *The President of the Projectors* (1631) ; Strode's *Floating Island* 3. 4 (1636) ; Newcastle's *Captain Underwit* 2. 3 (c. 1640) ; *A Projector being lately Dead*, which is a non-extant play mentioned in *A Collection of Judgements upon Sabbath-Breakers* (1636) ;[1] and Thomas Herbert's *Newes out of Islington* ; or, a *Dialogue very merry and pleasant betwixt a knavish Projector, and honest Clad, the Ploughman.* *With certain Songs of the late fall of the new Beare-garden* ; *and for the fall of Projectors* (London, 1641). And finally, *The Stage Player's Complaint*[2] (1641) has a passage worth quoting : ' For Monopolies are downe, Projectors are downe, the High Commission Court is downe, the Starre-chamber is downe, and (some think) Bishops will downe.'

[1] Fleay, *Biog. Chron.* 2. 339.
[2] Ashbee's reprint, p. 4.

BIBLIOGRAPHY

ACOSTA, JOSEPH. Natural and Moral History of the Indies, Grimeston's tr. London, 1604. (Hakluyt Soc., 1880.)

ACTOR'S Remonstrance, The. London, 1643. (Repr. by W. C. Hazlitt in Documents and Treatises Relating to the English Drama and Stage. Roxburgh Library, 1869.)

ADAMS, J. Q., Jr. Lucian's Vera Historia and Icaro-Menippus. Mod. Lang. Notes 21. 1–3.

ALLEN, H. F. A Study of the Comedies of Richard Brome, especially as Representative of Dramatic Decadence. Michigan dissertation. Stanford Univ. Press, 1912.

ALLIBONE, S. A. Critical Dictionary of English Literature, and British and American Authors. 3 vols. Philadelphia, 1859.

BACON, FRANCIS. Works. 2 vols. London, 1838.

BAETKE, W. Kindergestalten bei den Zeitgenossen und Nachfolgern Shakespeare's. Halle dissertation, 1908.

BALLMAN, O. Chaucer's Einfluss auf das Englische Drama im Zeitalter der Königin Elisabeth und der Beiden Ersten Stuart-Könige. Halle dissertation, 1901 (and Anglia, Vol. 25).

BARCLAY, JOHN. His Argenis Translated out of Latine into English; The Prose by Sir R. Le Grys, and the Verses by Thomas May. London, 1629.

BAYNE, RONALD. Lesser Jacobean and Caroline Dramatists. (Cambridge History of English Literature. Cambridge, 1910. Vol. 6, chap. 8.)

BEAUMONT and FLETCHER. Works. (Ed. A. Dyce.) 11 vols. London, 1843–6.

Bibliotheca Anglo-Poetica, or a Descriptive Catalogue of Early English Poetry. London, 1815.

Biographica Dramatica, or a Companion to the Playhouse (D. E. Baker, I. Reed, S. Jones). 3 vols. London, 1812.

BORMANN, H. Der Jurist im Drama der Elisabethanischen
Zeit. Halle dissertation, 1909.

British Museum Catalogue of Printed Books. London, 1882.

BROME, ALEXANDER. Poems. London, 1661.

BROME, RICHARD. Works. 3 vols. London, 1873.

BURTON, ROBERT. The Anatomy of Melancholy (Ed. A. R.
Shilleto). London, 1893.

CAREW, THOMAS. Poems (Ed. A. Vincent. Muses' Library).
London, n. d.

CARTWRIGHT, WILLIAM. Comedies, Tragi-Comedies, with other
Poems. London, 1651.

CHAPMAN, GEORGE. All Fools and the Gentleman Usher
(Ed. T. M. Parrott). Boston, 1907.

—— —— Works. (Ed. Swinburne and Shepherd). London,
1874–5.

Choyce Drollery, 1656, Merry Drollery, 1661, An Antidote against Melancholy, 1661 (Ed. J.W.Ebsworth). Boston,
Lincolnshire, 1876.

CIBBER, COLLEY. An Apology for the Life of Colley Cibber.
Written by Himself. With a List of Dramatic Authors
and their Works. 2 vols. 4th ed. London, 1756.

COKAYNE, Sir ASTON. Works (Ed. J. Maidment and W. H.
Logan). Edinburgh, 1874.

COLLIER, J. P. A History of English Dramatic Poetry to the
Time of Shakspere: and the Annals of the Stage to the
Restoration. 3 vols. London, 1879.

CORSER, THOMAS. Collectanea Anglo-Poetica, Manchester,
1860–83. Vol. 1.

CORYAT, THOMAS. Crudeties. London, 1611. (Repr. Macmillan,
1905.)

DEKKER, THOMAS. Dramatic Works. 4 vols. (Ed. John Pearson.)
London, 1873.

Dictionary of National Biography. 63 vols. London, 1885–
1901.

DODSLEY, ROBERT. Old English Plays. 4th ed. (Ed. W. C.
Hazlitt.) London, 1875.

DONNE, JOHN. Poems (Ed. G. Saintsbury. Muses Library).
2 vols. London, 1896.

ECKHARDT, E. Die Dialekt- und Ausländertypen des Älteren Englischen Dramas. (Materialien zur Kunde des Älteren Englischen Dramas. Vols. 27, 32.) Louvain, 1910, 1911.

FAUST, E. K. R. Richard Brome. Halle dissertation, 1887 (Also in Herrig's Archiv, Vol. 82.)

FLEAY, F. G. A Biographical Chronicle of the English Drama. 1559–1642. 2 vols. London, 1891.

—— —— A Chronicle History of the London Stage. 1559–1642. New York, 1909.

FORD, JOHN. Dramatic Works (Ed. A. Dyce). 3 vols. London, 1869.

FRIEDLAND, L. S. The Dramatic Unities in England. (Journal of English and Germanic Philology 10. 56). 1911.

GARDENER, S. R. The Personal Government of Charles I. London, 1877.

GENEST, JOHN. Some Account of the English Stage 1660–1830. Bath, 1832.

GLAPTHORNE, HENRY. Plays and Poems. 2 vols. London, 1874.

Glossographia by T. B. London, 1656.

Grolier Club Catalogue of Original and Early Editions. New York, 1905.

HALLIWELL, J. O. A Dictionary of Old English Plays. London, 1860.

HAZLITT, W. C. A Collection of Documents and Treatises relating to the English Drama and Stage.

—— —— Handbook to the Popular, Poetic, and Dramatic Literature of Great Britain. 3 series, supplements, and general index. London, 1867–89.

HEYWOOD, THOMAS. Works (Ed. J. Pearson). 6 vols. London, 1874.

HOWELL, JAMES. Epistolæ Ho-Elianæ (Ed. J. Jacobs). London, 1892.

JOHNSON, W. S. Ed. Johnson's The Devil is an Ass. (Yale Studies in English No. 29). New York, 1905.

JONSON, BEN. Works (Ed. W. Gifford and Col. F. Cunningham). London, 1875.

KOEPPEL, EMIL. Ben Jonson's Wirkung und Andere Studien (Anglistische Forschungen No. 20). Heidelberg, 1906.

KOEPPEL, EMIL. Brome's Queen and Concubine (In App. to Quellen-Studien. Quellen und Forschungen No. 82). 1897.

—— —— Studien über Shakespeare's Wirkung auf Zeitgenössische Dramatiker. (Materialien zur Kunde des Älteren Englischen Dramas No. 9). 1905.

KOCH, MAX. Rev. of E. K. R. Faust. Richard Brome (Englische Studien 12. 97).

KYD, THOMAS. Works (Ed. S. Boas). Oxford, 1901.

LAMB, CHARLES. Works (Ed. E. V. Lucas). 7 vols. London, 1903.

LANGBAINE, GERARD. An Account of the English Dramatic Poets. Oxford, 1691.

LODGE, EDMUND. Illustrations of British History, Biography, and Manners. 3 vols. London, 1838.

LOWNES, W. T. The Bibliographers' Manual of English Literature. 6 vols. London, 1857.

LUCIAN. Works. Trans. by H. W. Fowler and F. G. Fowler. 4 vols. Oxford, 1905.

MARMION, SHAKERLEY. Works (Ed. J. Maidment and W. H. Logan). Edinburgh, 1875.

MASSINGER, PHILIP. Plays (Ed. W. Gifford). 4 vols. London, 1815.

MANDEVILLE, Sir JOHN. Travels. London, 1900.

MAYNE, JASPER. The City Match (Hazlitt's Dodsley, Vol. 13).

MIDDLETON, THOMAS. Works (Ed. A. H. Bullen). 8 vols. Boston, 1885.

MURCH, H. S. Ed. Beaumont and Fletcher's Knight of the Burning Pestle. (Yale Studies in English No. 33). New York, 1908.

MURRAY, J. T. English Dramatie Companies. 2 vols. Boston, 1910.

Musarum Delicæ: or the Muses' Recreation, 1656. New ed. 2 vols. London, 1874.

NABBES, THOMAS. Works (Bullen's Old English Plays, 2nd ser.) 2 vols. London, 1887.

NEWCASTLE, Duke of. The Country Captain (Bullen's Old English Plays, Vol. 2). 1883.

Bibliography

139

NEWCASTLE, Life of, by Margaret, Duchess of Newcastle (Ed. C. H. Firth). London, 1886.

OLIPHANT, E. H. The Problem of Authorship in Elizabethan Drama (Modern Philology 8. 3).

PEPYS, SAMUEL. Diary (Ed. Wheatley). 9 vols. London, 1893–9.

PHILLIPS, Edward. Theatrum Poetarum Anglicanorum. London, 1875.

POTTS, THOMAS. Discovery of Witches in the County of Lancaster. Repr. from the ed. of 1613, with notes by J. Crossley (Chetham Soc. Vol. 6). Manchester, 1845.

PRICE, W. H. The English Patents of Monopoly. Boston, 1906.

RANDOLPH, THOMAS. Works (Ed. W. C. Hazlitt). London, 1875.

REYHER, P. Les Masques Anglais; Etude sur les Ballets et la Vie de Cour en Angleterre (1512–1640). Paris, 1909.

ROLFE, W. J. Ed. Two Noble Kinsmen. New York, 1883.

SAINTSBURY, G. Ed. Minor Poets of the Caroline Period. Oxford, 1905.

SCHELLING, FELIX. Ben Jonson and the Classical School. (Publications Mod. Lang. Ass., Vol. 13, no. 2.) Baltimore, 1898.

—— —— Ed. Ben Jonson's Timber. Boston, 1892.

—— —— Elizabethan Drama. 2 vols. Boston, 1908.

SCHWAB, H. Das Schauspiel im Schauspiel zur Zeit Shakespeares. Leipzig, 1896.

Shakspere-Allusion Book. A Collection of Allusions to Shakespere from 1591 to 1700 (Ed. John Munro). 2 vols. London and New York, 1909.

SHIRLEY, JAMES. Works (Ed. Gifford and Dyce). 6 vols. London, 1833.

Stage-Players Complaint. 1641. (In E. W. Ashbee's Facsimile Reprints 1868–72).

Stationer's Register. Transcript by E. Arber. 5 vols. London, 1875–94.

STRODE, WILLIAM. Poetical Works (Ed. B. Dobell). London, 1907.

SWINBURNE, A. C. Rev. Works of Richard Brome (Fortnightly Review, Vol. 57). 1892.

SYMMES, H. Les Débuts de la Critique Dramatique en Angleterre jusqu'à la Mort de Shakespeare. Paris, 1903.

SYMONDS, J. A. Rev. Works of Richard Brome (Academy 5. 304). 1874.

TENNANT, G. B. Ed. Jonson's New Inn. (Yale Studies in English, No. 34.) New York, 1908.

THOMPSON, E. N. S. The Controversy between the Puritans and The Stage (Yale Studies in English, No. 20). New York, 1903.

TOURNEUR, CYRIL. Plays and Poems (Ed. J. C. Collins). 2 vols. London, 1878.

WALLACE, C. W. Shakspere and the Blackfriars (Century Magazine 80. 5).

WARD, A. W. Richard Brome. (Dict. Nat. Biog.).

—— —— History of English Dramatic Literature to the Death of Queen Anne. 3 vols. London, 1899.

WHITE, A. D. The Warfare of Science and Theology. 2 vols. New York, 1910.

WINSTANLY, W. Lives of the Most Famous English Poets. London, 1687.

WINTER, DE. Ed. Jonson's Staple of News (Yale Studies in English, No. 28).

WOODBRIDGE, ELIZABETH. Studies in Jonson's Comedy (Yale Studies in English, No. 5). Boston, 1898.